Dr. Dorus Paul Rudisill is Professor of Philosophy and Religious Studies at Lenoir Rhyne College and Head of the Department.

Dr. Rudisill was born in Cherryville, North Carolina, and was educated at Lenoir Rhyne College, Lutheran Theological Southern Seminary, University of South Carolina, Hartford Seminary, and Duke University. Prior to his coming to Lenoir Rhyne College, he was minister to four Lutheran parishes in North Carolina. During his ministry he organized three congregations.

Dr. Rudisill has filled numerous appointments as lecturer and preacher during his years at Lenoir Rhyne College. He was a member of the Board of Trustees of the Lutheran Theological Southern Seminary for a number of years and served as a delegate to the National Council of Churches on two occasions.

Love

Activates and Acts

Love

Activates and Acts

by

DORUS PAUL RUDISILL, PH.D.

Poseidon Books, Inc.
New York, N. Y.

To

IONE,

PAUL,

SUZANNE,

and

BARBARA

ACKNOWLEDGMENTS

In the preparation of this book I have had the thoughtful suggestions of Dr. S. L. Schillinger, Pastor of St. Paul's Lutheran Church, Hickory, North Carolina; the Reverend J. A. Linn, who for a number of years was a missionary to Japan and more recently served Lutheran parishes in North Carolina; and Mrs. Albert Keiser, a former teacher at Lenoir Rhyne College. I am also deeply indebted to Dr. Laura Clayton, Dr. Inez Seagle, Dr. Joseph Glass, and Chaplain Louis Rogers, my colleagues at Lenoir Rhyne, for their constructive comments.

CONTENTS

PREFACE

It has been my good fortune to teach Christian Ethics for a number of years at Lenoir Rhyne College. I have invariably taught this course from the point of view of Evangelical Ethics. This little book is the outgrowth of my presentations and of discussions with students. It is designed to set forth the ethical foundation for decisions and actions of the Christian as his life is related to his own historical situation.

Evangelical Ethics has reference exclusively to the life of the Christian. It relates to nothing more or nothing less than the manner of life that the Christian should live in his redeemed relation to God. This is the undeviating point of view of the author of this book. Since this is the case, Evangelical Ethics is rooted genetically in God's revelation of Himself in the redemptive work of Christ.

Many writers distinguish between vertical and horizontal relationships. The vertical refers to the relation between God and man and the horizontal to man's relation to man. This distinction is valuable as long as it is understood to be a communicative device. If, however, the distinction indicates separable relationships, it is misleading. In Evangelical Ethics the vertical informs and energizes the horizontal. Thus, the vertical is necessarily and invariably the ground of the horizontal.

Evangelical Ethics, being a study of the life of the Christian, does not begin with a postulation of principles or maxims. This is to affirm that Evangelical Ethics is neither rationalistic nor dogmatic.

Evangelical Ethics does not begin by selecting a set of virtues, such as wisdom, courage, temperance, and justice to which man devotes himself with passionate energy to achieve the highest good. Such virtues may well fall within the scope of Christian experience.

Nor should Evangelical Ethics begin by identifying mortal sins, such as pride, gluttony, sloth, and avarice, and by contradicting these vices arrive at the virtues that should constitute Christian behavior. Evangelical Ethics must start with revelation, and must restrict itself to revelation. Reflection is restricted by this revelation.

I have selected *Love Activates and Acts* as the title for this book to indicate that God's love evokes and energizes Christian love and that Christian love expresses itself in action. It should be emphatically stated that this book has reference only to the life of the person who is committed to Christ. An attempt is made to express the meaning of this faith-relationship to areas of vital response. For instance, in dealing with revelation in Chapter I, I have in mind the Christian who has been brought to faith through the final revelation of God in Christ, but I do not have in mind the full scope of the idea of revelation. It is, therefore, imperative that the limitations of this analysis be kept in mind.

INTRODUCTION

THE EVANGELICAL POSITION

GOD IS LOVE and His love for man is absolute, absolute both with respect to its purity and completeness and with respect to its constancy and finality. Herein is the essence of revelation in Christ. In Christ is the New Covenant. His death is the seal of divine veracity, and God Himself could not break this seal without violating His integrity. This covenant is absolute; there is no halfway covenant here.

Responding faith, too, carries the quality of absoluteness, for faith indicates the presence of grace that has effected regeneration and reconciliation. And there is no halfway regeneration or halfway reconciliation. It is within these absolutes that the Christian lives, and it is within these absolutes that the Christian is edified by Word and Sacraments.

Since the Christian is a historical person, his decisions and actions are expressed within the situation in which he finds himself from moment to moment. The following comprise the essential elements of the situation in which the Christian lives. "You," the Christian, are the "I" in the situation.

3

1) THE SITUATION OF FAITH.

I believe that my Father has created me and all that
exists.

I believe that He continues to preserve me and His
created order.

I believe that it was His love that prompted Him to
create all things and to give me life.

I believe that His eternal love has never been absent
from me and will never desert me.

I believe that Christ is the Word of God.

I believe that Christ has died for me.

I believe that Christ was sinless.

I believe that He overcame death.

I believe that He is the living Lord.

I believe that the Holy Spirit has called me through
the Gospel.

I believe that my sins are forgiven by grace.

I believe that I belong to the communion of saints.

I believe that God will raise me from the dead.

I believe in the life everlasting.

These affirmations constitute a vital portion of my situation.

2) THE SITUATION OF CONSTRAINT.

I believe that I must not offend Him who has loved
me and given Himself for me.

I believe that I cannot sin with impunity.

I believe that I must love myself because God has given life to me and because I belong to Him.

I believe that I cannot injure my neighbor in any way without denying my faith in God.

I believe that my love for God can find expression in my love for my neighbor.

I believe that I should forgive my neighbor's offenses toward me as I am forgiven by my Father.

I believe that I must help my neighbor when he is in need.

I believe that I must respect God's created order, for this is His world.

These are among the constituents of constraint for me.

3) THE SITUATION OF UNIQUENESS.

I am a person.

I am unique.

I possess individuality.

I cannot be duplicated.

I live in this historical moment.

I live in this social situation.

I express my Christian commitments in the situation in which I live.

I cannot create the situations in which I make decisions.

I find every momentary situation a unique one.

I cannot remake situations nor can I predict future situations in which I will be involved.

I am a unique person and my situations are mine alone.

4) THE SITUATION OF COMPLEXITY.

I am a living organism in a physical universe.

I am subject to this physical environment in which I live.

I am in a world of persons.

I am a member of a social, economic, and political milieu.

I live among people who are immoral and anti-Christian.

I live among people who are honest, sincere, and well-meaning.

I am subject to disease and to the unpredictable assaults of sinful man.

I must make all my choices as a Christian within this complexity.

5) THE SITUATION OF AN UNEASY CONSCIENCE.

I find it difficult to discern what I should say and what I should do under the varying situations in which I find myself.

I cannot always do what I want to do because some persons attempt to frustrate my efforts.

I find that my decisions do not always fully express my Christian convictions.

I engage in corporate activities which offend my Christian sensibility.

I know that guilt belongs to me when I fail to activate my Christian faith.

I am smitten by an uneasy conscience.

6) THE SITUATION OF GRACE.

I am unworthy of the love of God.

I live under His holy love.

I am forgiven for Christ's sake.

I am a Christian through grace.

Here, also, affirmation must be forthright and incisive. The foregoing description comprises salient elements of the situation in which the Christian lives. However, these elements do not constitute a context. Context indicates something external. The Christian is a new creation, a new creation through the gracious work of God. As a new creation he stands in a new relationship of love. Such a relationship transcends external norms, and it may not be too much to say that it indicates identification. Love is communicative. And in the very outgoing of love there is an identification with the interest and welfare of the person who is loved. Christ has identified Himself with the frightful needs of man by His conquest over sin and death. The Christian's responding love indicates his identification with Christ's victory. Thus, decisions and actions of the Christian are

not governed by rules or principles of behavior, but are
motivated by this living, personal relationship. Love is not
only the fulfillment of the law, but also the motive for its
fulfillment. This relationship delivers the Christian from
the galling yoke of casuistry, moralism, expediency, and
conformity. He is not bound by anything that is external,
but is moved by constraining love. He is not perfect, but
the relationship is perfect. In this relationship, he continues
to be edified. He lives and moves in the historical situation,
but his life is anchored in God.

Chapter 1

REVELATION

IT IS IMPORTANT to keep in mind the limited scope of this treatise, which refers only to the life of the Christian. The wide scope of revelation is not being discussed here. Only that revelation that relates directly and exclusively to the evoked commitment of faith by the Christian is to be treated. This commitment by faith is generated by the act of God in the redemptive work of Christ. Hence, faith is not the product of human effort, but it is a divine gift because revelation is a divine act and faith is a motivated response. Christian faith is a verification of revelation. The Christian's awareness of his own faith is at the same time an awareness that he did not initiate this faith. Revelation, hence, is lifted out of the context of speculation. For the Christian, both the nature and the significance of revelation are to be seen from the point of view of faith.

A discussion of revelation from the point of view of Christian faith presupposes the reality of God Who enters into personal relations with man. And it presupposes, also, the nature of man as image of God who is thereby capable of

9

experiencing a personal relationship with God. Although
these presuppositions are logically basic to an analysis of
revelation, they are the essential elements of revelation
as well. It is through revelation that the personal relationship of God to man is ascertained, and it is through revelation that the Christian knows himself as image of God.
Thus, these two basic presuppositions are more than logical
postulates; they are the substance of revelation.

Revelation is not the consequence of man's reflections
upon himself or upon natural phenomena. Revelation is
God's activity. It is utterly impossible to explain with complete clearness why God revealed Himself, though we may
say that all His activity in relation to man stems from and
expresses love.

Any attempt to devise a term which represents God's
activity toward man is fraught with difficulties. Although
a precise definition of revelation will not be attempted here,
some things can be said about it with assurance. This will
suffice for our purpose. By pointing out some of the indispensable facets of revelation, one should be able to identify
it and to explore its implications for the life of the Christian.

One is on firm ground when speaking of revelation as
divine self-disclosure. Accent must be both on divine and
on self-disclosure, for revelation is a divine act, and it is also
the disclosure of the divine. The disclosure spoken of here
is not the disclosure of certain attributes of God. It is the
disclosure of God Himself. However, when an attempt is
made to speak of this disclosure, the verbalization is not
equivalent to the revelation itself. Man is keenly aware of
God as God reveals Himself. It is the very nature of God
in His encounter with man.

A closely related expression is divine self-affirmation.
Here again the accent is twofold: on the divine and on
self-affirmation. It is God affirming Himself. Affirmation,

then, stands in its own right without any corroboration beyond its own reality or without any justification beyond its own motive. It must possess this nature for the affirmation is not about something other than God; it is God affirming Himself.

A third emphasis may be expressed as divine self-impartation. Revelation goes beyond mere self-disclosure and mere self-affirmation. Revelation transcends information about God. Revelation involves in a very essential way the impartation of that which answers the need of man as he stands before God, both in his alienated state and in his reconciled status. Revelation is a divine succoring. Revelation is a revitalizing and nurturing activity of God. This vital aspect is often overlooked in the treatment of revelation.

Revelation is intentional. God wants to disclose, affirm, and impart Himself. Man has not found God by rational activity, nor has he arrived at a correct view of God by reflecting upon the nature of the physical universe. Revelation is not a consequence of human activity. Reflection begins with the confidence that the divine has come to man and that this revelation is self-aroused. Revelation springs from God's own nature, and it is pleasing to Him.

It is important to restrict this analysis. Only God's revelation to man is being considered. Whether God has revealed Himself to angels, to sentient creatures in other parts of our vast cosmos, to birds and bees and trees and other forms of life, is not under discussion here. God's revelation to man is all one has any right to proclaim. Revelation is God's encounter with man.

The next step in the attempt to say something significant about revelation is that it relates to sinful man. Grace and mercy are common words in the Christian vocabulary. They are meaningful terms only in reference to sin. Grace speaks of the unmerited favor of God to man, the sinner;

and mercy speaks of a divine forbearance toward man, the sinner. Both grace and mercy are known through disclosure, affirmation, and impartation of God. He desires to forgive. Forgiveness is far more than the erasure of an act. It is the restoration of community between God and man.

God's purpose in revelation is the redemption of man. The sole end of revelation is to establish and maintain a vital and harmonious fellowship between God and man and between man and man. Man is not a mere spectator beholding God. A spectator may stand speechless before a dazzling object or an awesome mystery. But the end of revelation is that man may say, "Abba," "Father."

Many theologians have affirmed that the Christian is under judgment and grace. This affirmation is misleading if judgment is related to the law that has been cancelled. This error has been too commonly made. It might be clearer to say that God's grace is a judgment upon the Christian rather than to say that the Christian is under judgment and grace. Grace judges the Christian in two ways. First, the very nature of grace is a judgment upon the Christian, for it indicates that the Christian is not in the favor of God because of his own goodness. Grace judges him to be unworthy of God's favor. Second, grace judges him to be the heir of God and a joint heir with Christ. So grace adjudges the Christian to be an unworthy heir, but an heir nonetheless.

For the Christian both the significance and the vitality of revelation have their source in Christ. He is the divine revelation. He is the final revelation. The only God the Christian knows is Christ. This is the central significance of the Incarnation. Revelation itself and the Christian's understanding of the content of revelation must begin with Him. In Christ is divine self-disclosure, in Christ is divine self-affirmation, in Christ is divine self-impartation, in Christ the Christian stands under the judgment of grace. And this

revelation is final. There will never be a revelation that
supersedes His succoring self-disclosure in Christ. God's
redemptive activity is final in Him. He and He alone is
the Word of God, for in Him is the final Word of Judgment
and the final Word of Grace. The Word of God is eternal,
but the Word became incarnate and dwelt among us. This
final Word is in the begining and He is unchangeable. Christ
as the final revelation is the Eternal Word Who became
historical. The living and eternal Word, as a historical
person, suffered and died for man's redemption.

A wrong approach to a conception of Christ is commonly
made. First, a delineation of the attributes of God is given.
Then, it is said that Christ manifested these attributes. The
conclusion to these two premises is that Christ is God.
The only proper approach proceeds from Christ Himself
as the final revelation. It is in Him alone and through Him
alone that the Christian can answer the question: "Who
is God?" The answer is not in the form of a definition. The
evangelical answer would involve the affirmations that God
is He Who has come to man redemptively in Christ, that
God is He in Whom a person may trust with absolute assurance, and that God is He Whose redemptive activity in
Christ is the ground of man's hope. And this is the ultimate
meaning of revelation. The only God the Christian knows
is He Who is revealed in Christ. Thus, a correct understanding of revelation must begin with the person and work of
Christ, and must discern its finality in Him.

Although revelation is final in Christ, it is unfinished.
Christian insight into the person and work of Christ must
be continuously related to the historical situation. The
Christian is continuously engaged in a twofold interpretation. On the one hand, he views the historical Christ in His
perfect relation to the Father and to man. On the other
hand, the Christian seeks to relate Christ's life and teachings

to his own historical situation. The Christian, in any given century or in any given culture, is engaged in relating to his own situation the eternal and unchangeable Word of God as revealed historically. It is in this sense that the final revelation is unfinished, and it is at this point that the Holy Spirit leads the Christian into all truth.

By reason of the continuous activity of the Holy Spirit, the Christian today should have deeper insight into the life and teachings of Christ than Christians of former generations. Nor is it too much to say that the Christian today should have a deeper insight into the application of the Word of God to his present social, economic, domestic, and cultural situation.

I have omitted from the discussion of revelation what has been called "general revelation." The Christian has been brought to faith through Word and Sacrament. He knows God through the forgiveness of sin. His faith is not derived from any other source. For apart from Word and Sacrament, he does not know God's final revelation in Christ. General revelation does not disclose, affirm, and impart God, nor does it bring redemption. The phenomenal world may arouse in man the sense of mystery, it may evoke a sense of amazement regarding its vastness and orderliness, and it may stimulate ecstatic awe. It cannot evoke repentance, effect peace, and promise hope. The heavens declare the glory of God to a believer. The psalmist exultingly wrote this in consequence of the redeeming activity of God as it expressed itself in the deliverance and preservation of His people. The heavens did not evoke this song of praise. He saw the glory of God reflected in the glory of the created order. The point is this: the psalmist did not see God in the sun, the moon and the stars; he saw the sun and the moon and the stars in God.

It is from the point of view of the final revelation of God

in Christ that the Christian interprets natural phenomena and the acts of God in history. He cannot, for example, read the Old Testament as a mere literary production. The creation of the world, the fall of man, the deliverance of the children of Israel, the message of the prophets, and the Messianic hope are interpreted from the vantage point of the final revelation of God in Christ. From Him, all other types of revelation derive their authentication and significance. From Christ, the Incarnate Word, interpretation goes out to revelation in nature and revelation in history.

SUGGESTED READINGS

AULEN, GUSTAF. *The Faith of the Christian Church*. Translated by Eric H. Wahlstrom and G. Everett Arden. Philadelphia: The Muhlenberg Press, 1948. Chapter III, 30-47.

BAILLIE, JOHN. *The Idea of Revelation in Recent Thought*. New York: Columbia University Press, 1956.

BRING, RAGNAR. *How God Speaks to Us*. Philadelphia: The Muhlenberg Press, 1962.

FARMER, HERBERT H. *God and Men*. Nashville: Abingdon-Cokesbury Press, 1947. Chapter IV, 96-118.

FARMER, HERBERT H. *Revelation and Religion*. New York: Harper, 1954.

FORELL, GEORGE W. *The Protestant Faith*. Englewood Cliffs: Prentice-Hall, Inc., 1960. Chapter II, 32-79.

HAAS, JOHN A. W. *What Is Revelation?* Boston: The Stratford Company, 1937.

NIEBUHR, REINHOLD. *The Nature and Destiny of Man*. New York: Charles Scribner's Sons, 1955. Part I, Chapter V, 123-149.

SODERBLOM, NATHAN. *The Living God*. London: Oxford University Press, 1933. Chapters VIII, IX, X, 264-306.

DISCUSSION QUESTIONS

Chapter I: REVELATION

1. Why is revelation basic to a consideration of Christian Ethics?

2. What is the relation of revelation to the inspiration of the Bible?

3. What is natural theology? What are its values and its inadequacies?

4. Can one know that God is love from general revelation?

5. Why is divine self-impartation important for an understanding of revelation through Christ?

6. Why can it be said that revelation in Christ is final revelation?

7. Distinguish between final revelation and unfinished revelation.

8. Does God continue to reveal himself? If so, how?

GOD IS LOVE

WHAT IS MEANT by the expression "God is love?" Does it mean that God is loving? Does it mean that God loves us? If something meaningful cannot be said about the affirmation, why is it used at all?

Many writers approach the study of God by way of His attributes. For example, one finds such expressions as "God is omnipotent," "God is infinite," "God is immutable." Let us take a look at these three expressions and compare them with the expression "God is love."

It is said that God is omnipotent. Is this statement definitive? Does omnipotent mean that God can do anything that He wills and that there is no limit to His power? If this is what is meant, the thought is terrifying. It would mean that God could make the sun go in opposite directions at the same time, or it would mean that God could make a triangle and a circle equal, or that He could make two plus two equal six. If all power is an attribute of God and this power is not related to His nature, then there is no limit to what God can do. Or does omnipotent mean that

18

all power belongs to God, having its source in Him? Omnipotence is God's omnipotence. The concept of Divine omnipotence derives its true meaning from one's concept of Deity rather than from the definition of omnipotence. Suppose it is said that the Devil is omnipotent. Obviously the omnipotence is a resource or an activity of malevolence. This distinction between omnipotence as an attribute of Deity and as an attribute of the Devil makes apparent the necessity of interpreting omnipotence in reference to him who possesses it.

It is said that God is infinite. Infinity can be defined in two ways. If the world is infinite, that is, if space and time are infinite, measurable extent and measurable duration are without limits. If this use of infinite is applied to God, God and the world tend to be equated. However, when saying that God is infinite, another meaning of the word is to be understood. Infinite here signifies transcendence or that God is not subject to or limited by measurability. But infinity, as it is applied to Deity, is also a frightening concept, just as omnipotence becomes a frightening concept when applied to Deity. It is frightening because a definition of transcendence would tend to remove God from the world of time and space and from man in the world of time and space. When it is affirmed that God is infinite, one's conception of infinitude derives its real meaning from one's conception of God and not from one's definition of infinitude. It is God Who is infinite.

God is immutable. Immutable indicates unchangeableness or unchangeability. Does it signify, then, that God is a static being? Rather, does it not mean that He is immutably God? He is never more and He is never less than God. He is always God. If one interprets immutable as unchangeable or fixed, is one not inconsistent when referring to God as the living God? The attribute immutable, thus, must derive its meaning from the nature of Him Who is immutable. Immutable, if it is to mean unchangeable, would make it very difficult if not impossible to conceive of Him as forgiving our trespasses.

God is love. Is love as a predicate to be placed on the same level as omnipotent, infinite, and immutable? Attributes such as omnipotence, infinity, and immutability are obviously negative terms. Omnipotence signifies that there is no limit to His power. But one cannot gain any conception of the meaning of unlimited. Infinite signifies without limit in another sense. Here also, one is without any definite idea of transcendence. Immutability is beyond conception since man is related to a world of change. These attributes along with other attributes, such as omniscience and self-sufficiency, must stand on a different level from love as it is used in the expression, "God is love." Love is not a predicate adjective like omnipotent, infinite, and immutable. Love signifies something more.

Love is not a negative term whose meaning man can barely comprehend, such as the concepts omnipotent, infinite, and immutable. It is a positive term that refers to the nature of God, for God is love. It is a positive term because it is the final revelation of God in Christ. Love is explicit in the Word of God Who became incarnate. Apart from the life, death, and resurrection of Christ, knowledge that God is love cannot be affirmed. Natural phenomena do not affirm this for man's existence is continuously in peril from which he finds no means of extrication. Man is in the middle of his predicament and cannot envisage any avenue of escape. The Word of God enters into the world of time and change to deliver man from the perils that threaten him and to bestow upon him that which makes life wholesome, meaningful, and full. This is the essence of salvation. It is because of His deliverance from evil and His bestow-

ment of wholeness that we know that God is love. His final
revelation in the life and work of Christ is the sole basis
for the affirmation that God is love. And it is in the light of
God's love that we understand His attributes. God, Who
is love, lovingly exercises His omnipotence, infinity, and
immutability.

The point can be demonstrated by reference to the
Apostles' Creed. "I believe in God the Father Almighty,
Maker of Heaven and earth." The accent is not on "Almighty" or on "Maker of Heaven and earth." Rather, the
stress is on "Father." It is my Father Who is the Maker of
Heaven and earth. Thus, the Christian affirms not that there
is a Creator Who is all-powerful, but that it is my Father
Who has expressed Himself in creating me and all that
exists. In like manner, the terms immutable and infinite
are to be understood. What is meant by these attributes is
that the Father is the source of all created objects; that
there is an unswerving determination to preserve all things
according to His will and power; that there is an unrelenting
determination to fullfill His purpose in creation; that He
is never absent from the historical process; that His intention
can never be frustrated by any alien force; and that He can
be depended upon as Father with absolute confidence. Thus,
one does not interpret God in terms of attributes, but
interprets attributes in the light of the conviction that He
is the Father.

Since the final revelation of God is Christ, it would
follow that to say "God is love" derives from the knowledge
that He has loved redemptively. Redemption by its very
nature takes account of the gravity of sin. This fact in
itself clearly indicates that His love is holy. God does not
condone evil but abhors it. His love is redemptively active
in the destruction of evil. It seeks this destruction in its
endeavor to recover man. If God's love were less than holy,

full restoration to fellowship would be impossible, for restoration of man does not occur without man's poignant awareness of his guilt from which redemptive love has set him free.

God's love seeks to evoke both repentance and faith. Repentance by its very nature signifies man's concurrence in God's judgment against sin. Repentance also is an act of faith, because repentance signifies turning away from that which God abhors to that which is holy in the sight of God. Repentance that does not turn toward God is no repentance at all; it is nothing more than a poignant despair. God's love is always holy. In fact, without being holy, it would not be love at all.

God's love is experienced by the Christian as grace, mercy, and long-suffering. Love itself is not divisible, but the Christian distinguishes among various experiences that have been evoked by God's love. He knows his own unworthiness and is aware that his own efforts do not remove this unworthiness. It is not at all surprising that a hymn writer uses the expression "amazing grace," for the experience of unmerited favor for Christ's sake is a startling event. Throughout his life the Christian is edified through Word and Sacrament, and this edification is paradoxical. On the one hand, the redemptive activity of Christ evokes a deepening sense of unworthiness; on the other hand, it evokes a heightened appraisal of that love that overcomes man's unworthinesss. It is in the very awareness of this deepening sense of unworthiness that gratitude for grace is increased. There is no gratitude for God's unmerited favor to man for Christ's sake apart from a keen awareness that Christ's redemption presupposes the heinousness of sin. The very gratuity of grace overwhelms, and it is a humbling experience. Thus, the revelation that God is love is progressively experienced. Paradoxically, the deeper the humility, the more exalted the divine grace.

God's mercy surpasses human understanding. It transcends man's conception of justice. Like grace, it is a divine gratuity. A sense of guilt, if it be a genuine experience and not a mere emotional aberration, is a personal accusation that carries with it a personal demand for punishment. In one's awareness of guilt, there is an accompanying concurrence in the rightness of divine judgment. If one feels that judgment is unfair or undeserved, he can never be aware of the meaning of mercy. The redemptive love of God in Christ embraces man's guilt, bears it as His own, and offers release. Here God reveals Himself. In this act of deliverance, God's love is known.

Not only does God's mercy relate to His forbearance, but it also relates to His providential care for His own creation. When the Christian prays for God's mercy, not only is he imploring God to be forbearing, but he is also expressing his need for God's diligent and continuous benevolence toward His created order.

Long-suffering cannot be rationally explained. How God endures with patience man's inhumanity toward man and man's infractions of the divine purpose is beyond understanding. But love abides and patiently seeks to overcome all forms of alienation of man from himself, from his neighbors, and from God.

Thus, the affirmation that God is love has its origin in God's acts of grace, mercy, and long-suffering. Little wonder that some writers have called this, "boundless love."

SUGGESTED READINGS

AULEN, GUSTAF. *The Faith of the Christian Church.* Translated by Eric H. Wahlstrom and G. Everett Arden. Philadelphia: The Muhlenberg Press, 1948. Chapters XII-XVII, 120-159.

BRANSCOMB, HARVIE. *The Teachings of Jesus.* Nashville: Cokesbury Press, 1931. Chapter X, 146-162.

FARMER, HERBERT H. *God and Men.* Nashville: Abingdon-Cokesbury Press, 1947. Chapter VI, 143-177.

NYGREN, ANDERS. *Agape and Eros.* Translated by Philip S. Watson. Philadelphia: The Westminster Press, 1953. Part I, Chapter I, 61-159.

OTTO, RUDOLF. *The Idea of the Holy.* Translated by John W. Harvey. New York: Oxford University Press, 1958.

DISCUSSION QUESTIONS

Chapter II: GOD IS LOVE

1. How does one know that God is love?

2. What are the basic manifestations of divine love?

3. Can one know that God is love by reflecting upon natural phenomena?

4. What is the relation of divine providence to the affirmation that God is love?

5. How would you distinguish between God's holiness and His love?

6. What is meant by the wrath of God? How can this be reconciled with the affirmation that God is love?

MAN

IT HAS BEEN said that the proper study of mankind is man. Though seemingly obvious, this dictum is misleading if "man" is interpreted too narrowly.

Let us take, for example, the study of geography. Geography encompasses the study of the continents, oceans, peninsulas, major river systems, mountain ranges, and the climate peculiar to each. Probably even more significant is the relationship of climate and topography to the basic needs of man: food, clothing, and shelter. Moreover, in studying the location of streams, mountains, and other natural barriers, it becomes rather clear that different cultures are related to the physical surroundings in which they are embedded. When combining the various aspects of physical geography, it is not difficult to see how one might say that man is what he eats. That is to say, the kind of food he eats, the kind of house he lives in, the kind of car he drives, and his material assets tend to shape his world view and crystallize the things he stands for and the things he opposes. It is not difficult, therefore, to arrive at an environmental interpretation of history from a study of man in relation to the earth on which he lives.

Let us turn now to the study of history. Here again one is studying mankind, for history revolves around the factors which contribute to the rise and fall of nations. One studies the manner in which ruler vies with ruler for domination, how one nation overcomes another nation, or how man has striven to free himself from tyrannical and despotic rule.

If one studies the history of art or literature, here again the "proper study of mankind is man," for in art and literature one tends to measure man according to his aesthetic and literary achievements. In literature, for instance, man's written contributions are a measure of his insights. It would seem that in every area of history man is studying man by turning his attention upon himself.

Sociology studies man in his group relationships. Sociology tries to explain the development of mores, conformity to conventional ways of thinking and acting, and conflicts within groups. I am aware that this is an over-simplification. The only point that I wish to make here is that in sociology man is also studying himself.

In anthropology man studies man, for anthropology attempts to trace the development of man from his earliest form to the present. It attempts to discover the forces inherent in man that effect cultural modifications. The fossil remains and artifacts of previous generations are scrutinized. Attempts are made to discover and trace the modifications of human anatomy and the growth of man's mastery of his environment. I am aware that this is an inadequate description of the wide area covered by anthropology, but I have said this merely to point out that, here too, man is studying man.

Psychology studies man with special stress upon his

responses to stimuli and to his total environment. Whether psychologists follow Watson and Dorsi in their behavioristic approach, Menninger in his analysis of the significance of death, the Gestalt theory that relates response to the syndromatic stimuli, Freud and his successors in psychoanalysis, or any other psychological point of view, man studies man.

The same is true in the fields of anatomy, physiology, histology, and other areas of biology. Knowledge is sought of the skeletal structure; of the circulatory, respiratory, digestive, and other systems; of the maladies that assault man; of curative medication and other types of therapy. In all of this, man studies man.

I would not for one moment disparage man's study of man. In fact, one should encourage wider and deeper study of man in the areas mentioned as well as in other important fields. The point I wish to stress is that knowledge gained about man from the study of geography, history, anthropology, sociology, psychology, biology, and other academic and scientific disciplines has not answered and cannot answer some of the most basic and insistent inquiries man makes about himself. Man has persistently asked three fundamental questions: Where did I come from? What am I doing here? Where do I go after death? Man seeks to know the origin of life, the purpose of living, and the end for which he is destined. These questions continue to preoccupy thoughtful writers in our own day. The very titles of some recent notable books are to the point. Reinhold Niebuhr entitled his Gifford Lectures at Edinburgh University in 1939 and 1941 *The Nature and Destiny of Man.* Robert L. Calhoun, a professor in the Yale Divinity School, has written a book entitled *What Is Man?* Lecomte du Nouy selected *Human Destiny* as the subject of his work. Also, there has been in recent years a wide-spread interest in

Existentialism. The works of Heidegger, Kierkegaard, Sartre, Jaspers, Camus, and other Existentialists are obsessed with the problem of human existence. And the Theology of Hope is rapidly gaining attention.

Augustine asserted that the only vital knowledge is knowledge of God. I am not sure that I understand all that Augustine meant by this affirmation, but he meant at least this: man cannot understand himself if he scrutinizes himself only in his various horizontal relationships. A proper understanding of man involves a knowledge of himself from the point of view of his Creator. Both the Old Testament and the New Testament speak of man from this point of view. "The proper study of mankind is man" indicates the horizontal approach. The Bible views man vertically.

If one applies this vertical approach to the study of man, some of its implications are immediately evident. I shall not attempt to relate the application of this vantage point to all areas of study previously mentioned. It will suffice to relate the vertical approach to history, psychology, and sociology.

History is to be understood as God's fulfillment of His purpose as He relates Himself to human events in time. History is more than the rise and fall of nations, the development and disintegration of distinct cultures, and the record of the achievements of man. History, in the Christian conception, is the record of God's condemnation and redemption of man. Although God Himself is timeless, He acts in the movement of time to realize His final purpose.

Again, the study of psychology should include man's encounter with God, Whose haunting presence is inescapable. Thus, man cannot fully understand himself if he examines only horizontal relationships. Man must be understood from above; that is to say, man must be understood to be a creature whose nature involves him in response to God.

The communal tendency which forms the subject matter of sociology reflects the inherent solidarity of man created as one humanity. The gregarious tendency of man can be explained in terms of the created oneness, a oneness in love. Gregariousness indicates more than mere herd instinct. It signifies that man does not find fulfillment in solitariness. His very nature is such that he seeks fellowship. On the other hand, man's tendencies toward fragmentation and isolation can be seen as indications of the presence of sin.

The horizontal interpretation of man is inadequate. Man cannot understand the origin of life, the meaning of life, and human destiny merely by looking at himself. He was created in the image of God and he cannot know this apart from revelation. He cannot know *who* he is apart from revelation.

That man was created in the image of God is a basic biblical doctrine. The acts of God both in the Old Testament and the New Testament affirm this. But what is meant by "image of God?" "Image of God" has been interpreted as corporeal likeness. It has been maintained that God has physical components. This would mean that God is located somewhere and that His corporeal components are measurable. But this denies both His transcendence and His immanence. Some writers have interpreted "image of God" as a rational faculty. Admittedly, this has merit. Memory, the ability to form rational judgments, to think, to communicate one's ideas, and to make value judgments are within the normal capacity of man. But this rational capacity does not coincide with the basic position of revelation regarding the nature of man.

Nor does the idea of transcendence do adequate justice to revelation. Admittedly, the idea of transcendence does have great merit. Man can transcend the present moment by recalling the past. Man can re-experience moments of joy and sorrow, aspiration and disappointment. He can project himself into the future. If one examines his activities at any moment, he will find that almost invariably every activity has a future reference. Every present act is an anticipation and, consequently, a means toward the realization of that which is anticipated. Each moment of existence relates the individual both to his past and to his future. Man is a transcending being. Man rises above himself when he considers the thoughts and actions that lie in his past or contemplates the future. Without this ability to transcend himself, it would be difficult to find any place in his nature for the experience of repentance. As a transcending creature, he does exhibit some likeness to the transcending God. But the idea of transcendence does not coincide with the basic position of revelation regarding the nature of man.

I should like to suggest that "image of God" signifies a relationship between God and man. It is that without which communion is impossible. And this is love. Man is created in love, to love, and for love. The loss of the image of God is alienation. Any form of sin is a breach of love, and alienation refers to the rejection of love. Redemption through Christ means the re-establishment of the alienated person in the law of nature and necessity. Redemption overcomes alienation by love and re-establishes man in love. The great commandment to love God and to love one's neighbor, the verbal expression of the law of nature and necessity, tends to confirm this. It would be difficult to interpret the message of either the Old Testament or the New Testament from any other point of view.

Understood in this way, the "image of God" does not refer to a faculty that man shares with God, but man's *relationship* with God. Who is man? The Bible does not attempt a description of man's rational, emotional, and volitional faculties, but it invariably speaks of man as sinner, forgiven sinner, son, and heir. It is man's *relationship* to God that is essential. When man responds to God's revelation in Christ he is in a love communion, and it is in this love communion that he knows the "image of God."

This is not to equate man's love with God's love. GOD IS LOVE. Man is a creature; he loves only in his knowledge that God is Love. Failure to love God is the very essence of alienation, and forgiveness signifies a revitalization of man through his response to God's love. Thus, man's likeness to God inheres in his created nature to which the gospel restores him.

It follows, therefore, that an understanding of the "image of God" derives from no other source than that of the final revelation of God in Christ. Through this revelation man comes to a knowledge of his true self.

SUGGESTED READINGS

CALHOUN, ROBERT L. *What Is Man?* New York: The Association Press, 1939.

ELERT, WERNER. *The Christian Ethos.* Translated by Carl J. Schindler. Philadelphia: The Muhlenberg Press, 1957. Chapter I, 23-48.

FARUQI, ISMAIL RAGI A. al. *Christian Ethics.* Montreal: McGill University Press, 1967. Chapter V, 157-192.

FORELL, GEORGE W. *The Protestant Faith.* Englewood Cliffs: Prentice-Hall, Inc., 1960. Chapter V, 127-165.

MATTSON, A. D. *Christian Ethics.* Rock Island: Augustana Book Concern, 1957. Chapter VI, 106-153.

NIEBUHR, REINHOLD. *The Nature and Destiny of Man.* New York: Charles Scribner's Sons, 1955. Part I, Chapter I, 1-25; Chapter VI, 150-177.

RAMSEY, PAUL. *Basic Christian Ethics.* New York: Charles Scribner's Sons, 1954. Chapter VIII, 249-325.

TITUS, HAROLD H. *Living Issues in Philosophy.* New York: American Book Company, 1964. Chapter IX, 143-162.

DISCUSSION QUESTIONS

Chapter III: MAN

1. Why is it important for man to understand his own nature?

2. What is the relation of one's conception of his own nature to his understanding of purpose and destiny?

3. Why should one study mankind in academic disciplines such as history, biology, sociology, and psychology?

4. Can man know his essential nature apart from revelation?

5. What do you understand by the phrase "image of God?"

6. Would you agree with the opinion that man lost his moral ability, but did not lose his natural ability, through sin?

7. On what ground can it be affirmed that every person is valuable?

LAW AND GOSPEL

WHAT IS MEANT BY LAW? Law has a variety of references, such as natural law, statutory law, moral law, Mosaic Law, and ceremonial law, and each has been variously interpreted.

When law is related to gospel, the Mosaic Law is commonly understood. But what is the Mosaic Law? Some writers have limited Mosaic Law to the Ten Commandments. Others have understood Mosaic Law to mean the entire Book of the Law with its minute requirements. Still others have included in it the development and interpretations of law over the centuries between Moses and Jesus.

Pharisaism promulgated a specific interpretation of the law. Paul who had excelled in Pharisaism knew law in its historical development and in its frightful demands. Obedience to law was the way of salvation. Works were done in order to achieve righteousness before God, and the curse fell upon anyone who failed to obey each and every demand that the law placed upon him.

But the Christian interpretation of law should not coincide

35

with the Pharisaic interpretation. Law, even as it appears in the Old Testament, must be understood in light of God's final revelation in Christ. Misunderstanding of law has frequently arisen because Christians have failed to see this.

Christian faith is postincarnation faith. "God was in Christ, reconciling the World unto Himself" (II Corinthians 5:19). Postincarnation faith is divinely evoked response to God's final revelation in the event of reconciliation. This final revelation may well be spoken of as the culmination of the preincarnation revelation. Christian faith affirms that God's work of redemption did not begin with the incarnation. It rejects the ancient heresies that the God of the New Testament is not the God of the Old Testament. It recognizes that there have been varying conceptions of God, but affirms that the same God has been actively revealing Himself throughout biblical history. Now that Christ is the final revelation, former conceptions of God must be reinterpreted in the light of this final revelation.

The point can be demonstrated by marking a distinction between nonfaith, Pharisaic faith, and evangelical faith. Nonfaith might express itself by a denial of the reality of God. It might express itself rebelliously by asking why God has any right to demand anything of man. Or again, nonfaith might express itself in a deliberate flouting of the will of God.

Pharisaic faith would express itself in an acknowledgment of legalistic demands. Righteousness would be achieved in precise obedience, and the curse of unrighteousness would follow any failure to obey.

Evangelical faith acknowledges the righteousness of God and the sinfulness of man. It is evoked by the gracious act of God in the work of redemption. Evangelical faith disclaims personal righteousness. It affirms that Christianity is not an achievement; it is a gift. Evangelical faith does not

seek righteousness before God by its own efforts, but it
makes a strong effort to live according to the will of God.
And this effort is an act within fellowship; it is also an act
of fellowship.

The law of God must be similarly interpreted. It must be
understood from the vantage point of evangelical faith. The
Christian does not know the law of God from the point of
view of nonfaith or Pharisaic faith, but he knows the law
of God from the point of view of evangelical faith.

A sharp distinction has been made between law and
gospel. Law is set in opposition to gospel and gospel in
opposition to law. Such a polarity disallows a reconciliation.
If law is paramount, then legalism is the consequence; if
gospel predominates, legalism is thereby negated or overcome. This sharp distinction calls for analysis.

When relating law to gospel, it is imperative that one
understand clearly the meaning of law. For instance, it is
said that Christ has cancelled the law and it is also said
that Christ fulfilled the law. These contrary affirmations can
be supported by New Testament passages. Furthermore, it
might be said that Christ cancelled the law by fulfilling the
law. What law did he cancel? What law did he fulfill?

What does the law mean for the Christian when he
relates law to gospel? Christians are told that they are not
under the law. In fact, they are told that they are dead to
the law. Again, they are told that love is the fulfillment of
the law. Is cancelled law the same as fulfilled law? Obviously
not. A distinction must be made between these two usages.

The word "law" has two distinct references. In the first
instance, law refers to the law of nature and necessity or
the law of love to be discussed shortly. This law has been
fulfilled by Christ. In the second instance, law relates to
righteousness through works and this law has been cancelled
by Him. This distinction is crucial, and in the clarification

of this distinction the relation between law and gospel becomes apparent.

Since man was created in love, for love, and to love, love is the law of life. This law of life is neither arbitrary nor alterable. Love is its own norm. It is not judged by anything other than itself. It is inherent in man's nature and as such it is necessary. Hence, it can be referred to as the law of nature and necessity, or the law of love.

Law that relates to nature and necessity is inherent in God. Man, who was created in the image of God, has his essential being in this law. But law that relates to legalistic demand does not derive from nature and necessity, but relates to defection from it. The law that relates to defection continues to aggravate this alienation, but the law that relates to nature and necessity continues to be the law of man's essential nature.

A distinction must be made between law as inherent in the nature of God and in the created nature of man, and law as a verbal formulation. If one begins with the formulated law, he finds that it is difficult to conceive of it as other than a demand and, consequently, there is a tendency to interpret law as a demand that does not derive from the nature of God Himself. On the other hand, if one begins by considering law as inherent in the nature of God and inherent in the created nature of man, then he is in a position to affirm that the law precedes any verbalization of it and that the formulation of it does not create the necessity of obedience.

The law of God inheres in God Himself. The formulated law is the necessary expression of Himself, and obedience thereto expresses man's created nature. The essential commandment is to love God and to love one's neighbor. This verbal formulation has a historical origin, but the law itself is prior to its historical origin. The law itself was prior to the formulation and the cause of its formulation. And it would have been the law for man even without its verbal formulation. The very nature of man created in the image of God and the very nature of man in personal relationship with his Creator established him within this law of his being.

To say that man is created by God is to say more than that his origin is from Him. It is to say that he is a person in personal relationship with his Creator, and this personal relationship involves him in love. This law, then, is not arbitrary because it relates to the nature of God and the created nature of man. Both the revealed nature of God and the revealed nature of man signify that law relates to nature. If it had expressed any form of arbitrariness, Christ's fulfillment of the law would have been the fulfillment of an arbitrary device. But He fulfilled the law, the law that is inherent in the very nature of God and in the created nature of man. He fulfilled this law because His love was perfect both with respect to His Father and to man.

We can affirm that law inheres in the nature of God and in the created nature of man from the historical point of view. The Ten Commandments, for instance, are preceded by the divine act of deliverance of the children of Israel. God intervened to deliver Israel from bondage in Egypt. Since God had taken the initiative and since it was His mighty work that delivered, this activity preceded the giving of the Ten Commandments which constrained obedience. His people could be motivated because they were persons created in the image of God. Thus, the Ten Commandments were not arbitrary demands because they expressed inherent moral relationships. If the Commandments had been in any way arbitrary, they would not have expressed nature and necessity, but they would have expressed arbitrariness.

It must be urged also that the keeping of the law to love by the children of Israel did not establish them in

righteousness before God; obedience signified the acceptance of God's covenant which He by His own initiative
established with His people. There was a failure to love God
before the verbalized commandment was given. Deliverance
of Israel came many years following the failure of the sons
of Jacob to love God and to love their brethren.

Because God had delivered the children of Israel no
other god should be worshipped. "I am the Lord thy God,
which have brought thee out of the land of Egypt, out of
the house of bondage. Thou shalt have no other Gods before
me" (Exodus 20:2-3). The commandment is restrictive.
However, it is His act of love that necessitates the restric-
tion. No other god had delivered them and only a god who
loved them would have delivered them. It is not the commandment *per se* that restricts; it is the revelation of the
God of deliverance that restricts.

The Old Testament clearly indicates that: 1) man had
failed to love according to his created nature; 2) God made
overtures to man to repent; 3) the call to repentance is predicated upon God's deliverance of His people; and 4) the
return to God is not effected by the obedience of man but by
his acceptance of God's forgiveness. It is not obedience to a
definitive demand that re-establishes man, but the effort to
obey is an acknowledgment of the covenant that God had
established with his people. The observance of the Festival
of the Covenant indicates this.

This understanding of law can be aptly applied to the
Ten Commandments. It is highly significant that the Old
Testament does not refer to the Ten Commandments as law.
These commandments were predicated upon God's act of
deliverance of His people from their Egyptian bondage and
upon His covenant with them at Sinai. The commandments,
therefore, were given to His people within this relationship,
and the observance of them was an indication of their

faithfulness within it. Obedience was not the work of righteousness, but it was in its very nature an acceptance of the righteousness of God. They were to obey Him within the relationship of deliverance. Disobedience was not an act in opposition to a commandment *per se,* but it was an indication of Israel's rejection of the relationship. Deliberate disobedience was a flouting of the covenant and an act of rejection of God Who delivered them. The frailty of man is acknowledged in the establishment of sacrifice, and the practice of sacrifice had reference to the righteousness of God Who always remained faithful to His covenant. Thus the Ten Commandments were not in opposition to the law of love. They were not an arbitrary imposition upon His people to restrict their behavior. They were a clear indication of the manner in which His people should live because they belonged to God.

For the most part, the commandments are given in the form of, "Thou shalt not." The prohibitions are not mere prohibitions. The negative manner in which some commandments are stated is a positive declaration of that which is abhorrent to God Who has delivered them and of that which is destructive of human relationships. Prohibition here does not signify a mere omission of a wrong act, for prohibition derives from the relationship. It is negative in form, but it is positive in its meaning.

This relationship of obedience to God's acts is made very explicit elsewhere in the Old Testament.

> And the Lord said unto me, Arise, take thy journey before the people, that they may go in and possess the land, which I sware unto their fathers to give unto them. And now, Israel, what doth the Lord thy God require of thee, but to fear the Lord thy God, to walk in all his ways, and to love him, and to serve the Lord

thy God with all thy heart and with all thy soul, to keep
the commandments of the Lord, and his statutes,
which I command thee this day for thy good
                                       (Deuteronomy 10:11-13).

Requirements here are not arbitrary demands because God's
firm intention to fulfill His promise is the impelling motivation. The keeping of the requirements would express their
reverence for Him Who had sworn to preserve them.

Micah expresses the same relationship between requirements and God's acts.

> Oh my people, what have I done unto thee? and where-
> in have I wearied thee? testify against me. For I
> brought thee up out of the land of Egypt, and redeemed
> thee out of the house of servants; and I sent before
> thee Moses, Aaron, and Miriam. O my people, remem-
> ber now what Balak king of Moab consulted, and what
> Balaam the son of Beor answered him from Shittim
> unto Gilgal; that ye may know the righteousness of
> the Lord. Wherewith shall I come before the Lord, and
> bow myself before the high God? shall I come before
> him with burnt offerings, with calves of a year old?
> Will the Lord be pleased with thousands of rams, or
> with ten thousands of rivers of oil? shall I give my first-
> born for my transgression, the fruit of my body for the
> sin of my soul? He had shewed thee, O man, what is
> good; and what doth the Lord require of thee, but to
> do justly, and to love mercy, and to walk humbly with
> thy God (Micah 6:3-8)?

The accent is on "He hath shewed thee, O man, what is
good;" but not on "requirement." God's faithfulness, God's
acts that transcend legalistic justice, God's abiding love in

spite of His children's rebelliousness constitute "shewed thee what is good." The context in which this passage occurs clearly indicates this. Requirement is thereby motivated. Requirement therefore must not be construed as a legalistic demand. Requirement refers to activities of His people that express their relation to God. Without this expression, they would be rejecting their God.

One might reverently ask, "Who is God?" "God" is merely a word, a syllable. "God" has had various meanings. I have observed elsewhere in this book that one can love God only in the knowledge that God is love. Here I should like to say that one can will "To do justly and to love mercy and to walk humbly with thy God" only as he knows that God is worthy of reverential respect. One can never "Do justly and love mercy and walk humbly with thy God" simply because some higher power demands it. Without a reverential respect for God it would be impossible for anyone to attempt "To do justly and to love mercy and to walk humbly with thy God." "He hath shewed thee what is good" is the accent in this passage. It is knowledge of what God has done for his people that causes Micah to implore God's people to make this moral response. This passage must never be interpreted legalistically. It is interpreted legalistically when the accent is upon requirement. Here, requirement is lifted out of a legalistic framework and it is centered in a moral relationship. It is hortatory since it is Micah's plea to his contemporaries, but it is also an imperative since it indicates an essential moral relationship. "To do justly and to love mercy and to walk humbly with thy God," is, after all, a parallel of the great commandment to love God and to love one's neighbors.

The same sequence is seen in the call to obedience of the Christian. This call is in the person and work of Christ. The call of the gospel is preceded by the work of redemp-

tion. It is a call to wholeness of life, and the call to wholeness
of life is the voice of love addressed to man who is created
for love and to love. This law of God cannot be arbitrary,
for the law to love could never be abandoned without a
denial of the creative nature of man and without a denial
of the very nature of the final revelation of God in Christ.
The Christian is not delivered from this law, but he is re-
established in it through the forgiveness of sin. The forgiveness of sin reaffirms man's nature. This law of God is not
in opposition to His nature; it is an affirmation of His nature.
Obedience, hence, is not a meritorious act. Obedience is an
act of faith in Him Who has returned him to fellowship
through the forgiveness of sin.

The call to obedience is a call within a faith relationship.
Paul called upon the Roman Christians to present their
bodies a living sacrifice on the basis of the mercies of God
(Romans 12:1). They could not present their bodies as a
living sacrifice if they were not under the mercies of God.
And the mercies of God are not exceptions to His nature,
but they are expressions of that nature as revealed in Christ.
The mercies of God call to man. Obedience is an act of trust
and adoration. Obedience is an act within this relationship
to God. Obedience indicates an acceptance of God Who is
love, and of one's self created in love, for love and to love.

The gospel, therefore, is not antithetical to this law of
love. The gospel is predicated upon man's failure to love
God and to love his neighbors, and the gospel is predicated
upon God's act of love in the incarnation. The gospel is
cradled in the law of love. As such it is not antithetical to
law, for there would never have been a gospel if love had
not been the law of life. The good news of the gospel is that
God in the person of His Son has delivered me in order that
I might be His. To be His is to be in His love and to live
in love. The gospel does not oppose this law of God; the

gospel reaffirms this law.

Since the law is inherent in the nature of God and the created nature of man, the law is good. Law that does not express the revealed will of God or law that is contrary to His will would not be related to man's accountability. It might be said that casuistry as it was developed within Judaism is unrelated to man's accountability. The law itself is good, but man is sinner. Man turned away from and continues to turn away from the law that is good. Hence, the law that is good relates itself to man as sinner and, the law that is good becomes for man the law unto sin and death. Now the law that is inherent in the nature of God and the created nature of man expresses a demand for righteousness that the sinner cannot attain through his own works.

When Paul says that Christians are not under the law, he is not referring to the natural and necessary law of love. Law here has a different reference. It is not inherent in either the nature of God or in the created nature of man. It refers to law that prescribes standards for righteousness. Strict adherence to these demands would result in Divine approval, but defection from these demands would bring God's judgment upon the offender. It is obedience or disobedience to definitive demands that determines respectively man's righteousness or unrighteousness. Paul sternly rejects this use of law and vigorously declares that Christians are delivered from this meaning of law. He goes so far as to affirm that any act done to obtain righteousness puts one under the demand of the entire law. He affirms that if one submits to circumcision as a meritorious act he is under the law with respect to every legalistic demand. Christians are not under this type of law; this law has been cancelled. This law has nothing to do with the Christian and the Christian has nothing to do with it.

It would be contrary to the Christian's conception of God
to urge that He demands anything of man that does not
derive from His nature as love. It would be equally contrary
to the Christian's conception of God to urge that He demands anything of man that would be to man's detriment.
When the Christian examines the Sinaitic law, it is necessary
to locate this law within grace since the law is a gracious
act of God and not an arbitrary demand. This is precisely
the point that is made in the Epistle to the Galatians.

> And this I say, that the covenant, that was confirmed
> before of God in Christ, the law, which was four
> hundred and thirty years after, cannot disannul, that
> it should make the promise of none effect. For if the
> inheritance be of the law, it is no more of promise;
> but God gave it to Abraham by promise
> (Galatians 3:17-18).

The works of the law construed apart from grace is a
curse. "For as many as are of the works of the law are
under the curse: for it is written, cursed is every one that
continueth not in all things which are written in the book
of the law to do with them" (Galatians 3:10). The law itself
is not a curse. The curse lies in the pride of man who seeks
his justification by his works. Since his works fall short of
the demands of the law, the law accuses and condemns.
And the law tends toward the aggravation of sin. The law
as such is not a curse, but it becomes a curse when obedience
to it is a work of righteousness. When righteousness is sought
through obedience to sheer legalistic demand, unrighteousness is the consequence. This Sinaitic law was given within
the context of grace, for it was not an instrument to continue
man's alienation from God; it was given within the covenant
of grace. To reiterate, the law itself was not a curse, but

the misconstruction of it became a curse. Paul sharply states that Christ has delivered us from the curse of the law, but he does not say that Christ has delivered us from the law of love.

Man's nature has been vitiated because of sin. The law of love continues to have respect for man's moral nature. The law that relates to nature and necessity now becomes the moral demand that relates to fallen nature. Since this is the case, the moral demand not only exposes sin, but it also becomes the occasion for deeper rebellion.

The distinction between law that is inherent in the nature of God and in the created nature of man and law that has reference to legalism must be clearly marked. The significance of law as it relates to nature and necessity is not the same as law that relates to legalism. The former use of law relates to that which is inherent in the nature of God and in the created nature of man and, consequently, can never be cancelled. The latter usage relates to work righteousness and, consequently, this law can never be fulfilled.

Law that relates to legalism is cancelled by the death and resurrection of Christ, but the law that relates to nature and necessity was fulfilled by Him. The Christian is not under legalistic law. He is justified by faith, and justification by faith secures him within the law of nature and necessity.

The law of love, the law of nature and necessity, signifies life. The very essence of love is vital and dynamic fellowship. Christ's fulfillment of the law relates to the restoration of man to this vital and dynamic relationship. Forgiveness indicates this.

Law as it relates to legalism does not restore life. It not only points to the predicament of man, but aggravates the extremity of his situation. Declaration of this law may awaken despair if the sinner seriously hears it. Man sees his inability to keep this law through his own efforts. He

is a legalist and he knows the futility of his efforts. Or the
declaration of this law, if the sinner seriously hears it, may
result in pride. Pride is a false evaluation of his own ability
and, consequently, deceives him. His efforts to keep this
law involve him in a deeper alienation. He can never, by
his own efforts, restore himself to the law of nature and
necessity, though he may believe himself capable of
doing so.

Finally, the Bible does not declare God's judgment against
sin as a single declaration. The declaration is invariably
related to the call to repent. Repentance itself signifies the
willingness of God to forgive. Forgiveness, if accepted, lifts
man out of sin and death and secures him in the law of
nature and necessity. The gospel by its very nature is a
proclamation that speaks of God's redemptive act on behalf
of sinners. The proclamation of the gospel relates sin and
death to the law of nature and necessity. In so doing, law
is not in opposition to gospel, but the gospel is cradled both
in the law of nature and necessity and in sin and death.
The Christian is not under sin and death even though he
be imperfect, for he is within the law of nature and necessity by grace.

SUGGESTED READINGS

AULEN, GUSTAF. *Church, Law, and Society.* New York: Charles Scribner's Sons, 1948. Chapter IV, 56-74.

BONHOEFFER, DIETRICH. *Ethics.* Edited by Eberhard Bethge. New York: The Macmillan Company, 1955. Part II, Chapter I, 271-285.

BRANSCOMB, HARVIE. *The Teachings of Jesus.* Nashville: Cokesbury Press, 1931. Chapter XII, 179-194.

CAVE, SYDNEY. *The Christian Way.* New York: Philosophical Library, Inc., 1949. Part I, Chapter VI, 122-133.

ELERT, WERNER. *The Christian Ethos.* Translated by Carl J. Schindler. Philadelphia: The Muhlenberg Press, 1957. Chapter II, 49-76.

FLETCHER, JOSEPH. *Situation Ethics.* Philadelphia: The Westminster Press, 1966. Chapter I, 17-39.

HARKNESS,GEORGIA. *Christian Ethics.* New York: Abingdon Press, 1957. Chapter II, 32-49.

MARSHALL, L. H. *The Challenge of New Testament Ethics.* New York: Macmillan and Company, Ltd., 1956. Chapter VII, 216-243.

NIEBUHR, REINHOLD. *The Nature and Destiny of Man.* New York: Charles Scribner's Sons, 1955. Part I, Chapter I, 265-300.

RAMSEY, PAUL. *Basic Christian Ethics.* New York: Charles Scribner's Sons, 1954. Chapter II, 46-91.

DISCUSSION QUESTIONS

Chapter IV: LAW AND GOSPEL

1. What is meant by law as inherent in God and inherent in man's created nature?

2. Are all laws in the Old Testament of equal value and permanence? Are the laws in Exodus 21-23 on the same level as the Ten Commandments in Exodus 20?

3. How can it be said that Christ both fulfilled and cancelled the law?

4. How is the law a schoolmaster to bring us to Christ (Galatians 3:24)?

5. Will the law to love God ever be abrogated? What is meant by law here?

6. Can man fully obey the law of love? If not, is he forever under judgment?

7. In what sense can it be said that the Gospel is not antithetical to the law of love?

FAITH

No ONE IS good enough to be a Christian. No one becomes a Christian by being good. One is a Christian through grace, and grace has reference both to the plight of man from which he cannot set himself free and to God's gift of His Son Whose redemptive act is final. The Christian strives to live the good life. He is edified within the fellowship of grace, but this growth does not indicate that he is more Christian.

At this point, I should like to relate an experience. I had made an appointment with a friend to meet him at a hotel. As I walked to the hotel, I passed by a church that had a bulletin board in front of it. The question on this bulletin board was, "Are you sure that you are a Christian?" When I arrived at the hotel, my friend was not there. He had been unavoidably delayed. While I was waiting for him, I reflected for some time upon the question, "Are you sure that you are a Christian?" I visualized many people walking by the bulletin board and reading the question. I imagined that some read the question and were indifferent and that

some others read the question and rebelled against it. I also
imagined that some persons read the question and inaudibly
answered, "No." They said to themselves, "I am not good
enough to be a Christian. I would like to be a Christian,
but I know my own imperfections, even my own gross
failures." These persons read the question and found in
themselves no basis for an affirmative answer. Perhaps others
read the question and inaudibly answered, "Yes. I live a
good life, I am honest and sincere, and I know that I am
better than some other people whom I know."

I continued to reflect. Can I know that I am a Christian
through introspection, through appraising my own failings
or my own good behavior? Can man ever know that he is
a Christian by looking at himself? I concluded that one
knows that he is a Christian by looking away from himself
toward what God has done for him. God declares that I am
Christian through the forgiveness of my sin. He declares
this through Word and Sacrament. He declares this through
His effectual grace. I can know that I am a Christian in the
certitude that He brings to me in responding faith. When
I look at myself, I find neither despair nor pride. Despair
is overcome by grace, and pride is vanquished by gratitude.

Permit me to stress this conclusion by referring to an
affirmation by a renowned minister who said that man has
fellowship with God on the basis of sin. This affirmation
startled me. As I reflected upon it, I saw its value. Fellowship is not on the basis of human goodness for no one is
good enough to be a Christian. It must be on the basis of
sin because man never commends himself to God in such
a way as to merit fellowship with Him. Being a Christian
is not an achievement; it is a gift!

Even so, the Christian strives for perfect imitation of
Christ. But this striving is in actuality a responding effort.
It is not he who strives, although he may be aware of his

experience. It is the effectual striving of God in him. The Christian continues to repent. His repentance, though, is not his own; it is his responding act within the fellowship of faith. Repentance indicates trust, and trust is continuously evoked through Word and Sacrament. Every experience whether it relates to emotion, will, or deed finds its origin in God's initiative. To be a Christian is to be willing to be possessed by God or, to put it differently, to be a Christian is to live in His love.

It follows that the greatest possession of the Christian lies in his willingness to be possessed. It would seem to me that this is the very core of the evangelical idea of justification by faith. Faith is not something that a Christian holds; it is his willingness to be held in the love of God. It is similar in its nature to conviction. The expression is heard quite often that a man has deep conviction as if this conviction were something that he held. A conviction that a person holds, if he holds it, is not worth holding because this would signify that he could release it if he willed to do so. Convictions grip the person and are tenacious. The Christian accepts God's love for him. And this issues in Christian living. Faith is not primarily something that one has or possesses; it is the strong conviction by the Christian that he is possessed by God. This is what is meant when he prays, "Our Father, Who art in Heaven" or when he says, "I believe in God, the Father, Almighty." To acknowledge God as Father implies our acknowledgment of ourselves as His sons.

Two incorrect analogies of faith that I have heard will serve to accent this point. Faith has been likened to a stalwart man with his arms extended at full length and tenaciously holding onto God Who is above. The grip of human faith is not strong enough for that. A better analogy of faith would be that of the relaxed mood of a child as it

is held in the arms of its mother during a moment of peril.
Faith is not so much tenacity as it is relaxation. It is a kind
of reckless abandonment of the self because of the conviction that God graciously acknowledges him as His child.

Again, faith has been likened to a child who holds his
father's hand as the two cross a busy street. Imagine an
emergency. The father attempts to pull the child to safety.
The grip of the child gives way and disaster follows. But
faith does not hold God. The analogy should be stated in
this way. The child willingly allows his hand to rest in the
grip of the father as the two cross a busy street. An emergency arises. All the strength of the father's arm is trans-
ferred to the child. The result is that the child is secure in
the tenacity of his father's grip. Christian faith is not something that the Christian possesses; it is his willingness to
be possessed in the love of God.

Luther expressed this point of view in his explanation of
the clause, "Thy Kingdom come" in the Lord's Prayer. He
said that, "The Kingdom of God comes indeed of itself,
without our prayers; but we pray in this petition that it may
come unto us also." To pray, "Thy Kingdom come" expresses
a will to live under the kingly rule of God, and it signifies
that he can live under the kingly rule of God because the
kingdom belongs to God.

Because this is the real essence of faith, it would follow
that the Christian is neither a pessimist nor an optimist.
The pessimist observes man's inhumanity to man, physical
suffering, and the inevitability of death. He looks at the
ugly and seamy side of life. His mood is that of frustration,
and his efforts to rectify or even ameliorate the human plight
are paralyzed by a sense of futility. Optimism, on the other
hand, may tend to overlook the ugly and seamy side of
life by concentrating its focus upon that which is beautiful
and good. The optimist would tend to overestimate the

ability of man to secure his own progress or development, and it could easily result in his belief that he is equal to the problems of life. The Christian is not an optimist for he does not overestimate the value of his own efforts.

The mood of the Christian is joy. He is realistic in that he knows that moral and physical evils abound in the world. He does not turn his eyes away from the human predicament, but he visualizes the Cross as erected in its very midst. The final Word for him is not futility but redemption. In this vision his efforts are released. He proclaims his sturdy witness to God's redemptive activity by exerting his efforts on behalf of God's children. Christian joy is not an emotional ecstasy; it is a joyful confidence in the redemptive activity of God and a joyful communion with Him through service to his fellowman. To rejoice in the Lord is essentially a rejoicing in His redemptive love, and this rejoicing is more than an emotional experience because it involves a serviceable activity in response to this conviction.

Faith glorifies God. Without trust it is impossible to give glory to Him. Faith bows in humble amazement before the boundless love that redeems, and it adores and gives thanks. Faith extends its hands in humble supplication to this boundless love that it may find in it the energy to do the will of God. And the highest glory that can be given to God is the acknowledgment of Him as God and the obedience that expresses itself in willing effort to imitate Him as He has revealed Himself in Christ. To glorify God is to live as His son, and this is the ultimate expression of faith.

SUGGESTED READINGS

AULEN, GUSTAF. *The Faith of the Christian Church.* Translated by Eric H. Wahlstrom and G. Everett Arden. Philadelphia: The Muhlenberg Press, 1948. Chapter II, 22-29.

BRUNNER, EMIL. *Faith, Hope, and Love.* Philadelphia: The Westminster Press, 1956.

EBELING, GERHARD. *The Nature of Faith.* Translated by Ronald Gregor Smith. Philadelphia: Fortress Press, 1967.

FORELL, GEORGE W. *The Protestant Faith.* Englewood Cliffs: Prentice-Hall, Inc., 1960. Chapter I, 1-32.

HARRINGTON, JOHN B. *Essentials in Christian Faith.* New York: Harper and Brothers, 1958. Chapter VII, 91-107.

SCOTT, ERNEST F. *The Ethical Teaching of Jesus.* New York: The Macmillan Company, 1949. Chapter IX, 66-70.

WEATHERHEAD, LESLIE D. *This Is the Victory.* Nashville: Abingdon-Cokesbury Press, 1941. Chapter III, 59-71.

DISCUSSION QUESTIONS

Chapter V: FAITH

1. How is faith evoked?

2. What is the difference between Christian faith and the faith of a scientist?

3. What is meant by justification by faith? Does justification signify imputed righteousness?

4. What is the relation between faith and works? Do works have anything to do with justification?

5. What is the distinction between faith as assent and faith as trust?

THE CHRISTIAN'S LOVE

IN CHAPTER FOUR on "Law and Gospel," some comments were made on the commandment to love God and to love one's neighbor. It is necessary to refer to this commandment again in order to emphasize some aspects that have not been treated.

"Thou shalt love the Lord thy God" is often interpreted as an imposed demand. Demand is often made to signify direful threat if the demand is not kept. But this is to misunderstand this first and greatest of commandments. "You must love God with all your being or you will go to hell" is the usual interpretation. What do we mean by "must"? Is it a demand with an attached threat? Or is "must" an expression of necessity which is rooted in the nature of man as a being created in the image of God?

This commandment to love God respects man's created nature and the relationship that this nature implies. Man, created in the image of God, is by nature capable of loving God; otherwise the commandment itself would be immoral. The commandment relates to man's capacity and expresses a necessity of his being. To state the point differently, this

58

commandment is in reality a definition of man's nature and not a command or a demand which is foreign to it. Man must love God if he expresses the full dimension of himself. Thus, the command to love God is not an arbitrary demand imposed upon man. It is definitive of man's true nature. If we interpret this commandment from the point of view of threat, the motivation for keeping it is fear and the emotion of fear does not evoke the response of love. For a command that rests upon threat can never evoke the response that it seeks. Love for God is a response to His nature and to His overtures. If the commandment is looked upon as grounded in God's knowledge of our created nature and in His knowledge that man is true to his own nature when he loves his Creator, then the commandment to love Him is highly moral. One must love God if he is to be his authentic self.

This interpretation of the commandment does not thereby remove the element of threat. But the threat is not an adjunct to the command nor is it the motive for obedience. "Threat" also inheres in the very nature of "must." Let me give an analogy. "You must breathe." That is to say, you must breathe if you desire to live. The threat involved in this is that if you do not breathe, you will die. In like manner, one must love God. If one does not love Him, he thereby becomes involved in alienation.

The Christian's love is a response to God Who is love. This being the case, the Christian's love is a unity that may be said to express itself as love of God, as love of one's self, and as love of one's neighbor. Love of God is meaningless apart from love of one's self and love of one's neighbor.

To love God is to love what God is. He has revealed Himself to be love, so to love God is to love "love." This is not a play on words; it is an actuality. It is another way of saying that to love God is a judgment of value. This value judgment derives from God's revelation of Himself in the final revelation through Christ. In Him the essence of His reality is revealed and through Him the superlative value of God is declared. And it may be added that this is the very essence of sovereignty. The sovereignty of God is not to be found in notions of omnipotence, immutability, infinity, or any other attribute. It inheres in love because it is love that acts omnipotently; it is love that gives meaning to immutability; and it is love that indicates His boundlessness.

To love God is to be interested in God's purpose for man and for His world. To affirm one's love for God and at the same time not to have a vital concern for the objects of divine love is obviously an inconsistency. Man's love of God is a vital element in God's redemptive purpose and an active participant in its realization. This interest and participation lifts love of God above mere affection. One loves God in the labors of his hands as man understands these activities as an expression of vocation.

Love of God signifies a giving of oneself to Him. Giving here signifies commitment, but it does not signify any form of exhaustion. There is a giving of one's self, as in evil activities, that results in both physical and moral deterioration. But there is a giving of one's self that enlarges the communication both in width and depth and at the same time enriches the content of that which is being communicated. In giving one's self in love to God, the chalice is continuously enlarged and the flow of dedication is enriched. It is from this point of view that the Christian understands reward because reward is not the reward of something one may behold as he may behold an object in his hand, but it is an enrichment of that devotion which he has expressed. The reward of generosity is a broader and deeper sense of generosity; of humility, a deeper humility. Love of God, as a giving of one's self, is an enlargement and an enrichment of oneself.

Love of God can be looked upon in a very practical way. It signifies hearing. Revelation, as we have observed, involves self-disclosure, self-affirmation, and self-impartation. The Christian has heard. Hearing involves something more than sound. It is insight and response. Through the gospel the Christian has been illumined regarding God's aversion to evil and of His regard for holiness, and this illumination continues in his life through the activity of the Holy Spirit. In loving God, the Christian seeks to hear what the gospel has to say to him. Luther expressed this in his explanation of the commandment to keep the Sabbath Day holy. He said that this commandment is kept by hearing and willingly learning the gospel. Hearing the gospel is a life-long activity of the Christian.

On the other hand, hearing involves listening to the world in which the Christian lives, the world of sin and death. It is very difficult to exaggerate the plight of man as he experiences privation, discrimination, suffering, and the inevitability of death. Apart from the hearing of the Word of God, the Christian does not see an elimination of these perils. But it is from this Word that he can speak to these perils with triumph. Menaces to life do not constitute finality. In the midst of life we are in death, but the death of Christ has passed the sentence of death upon death. The Christian's actions for social, economic, and domestic benefits do not spring from a mere interest in making life tolerable or merely happy. They are expressions of his confidence in the triumph of the Word of God.

Love of God signifies reflection. Reflection, thus, must spring from both the hearing of the Word of God and the cry of man. This is the real crux of Evangelical Ethics. How does the Christian who hears the Word of God relate himself in daily activities and in a variety of relationships to his fellowman? Love to God involves him in loving his neighbor.

Piety must not be divorced from morality.

To love God is also to love one's self. Love of one's self expresses the value that God has given to him in creation. It is not derived from any other source. In loving one's self, one accepts God's evaluation of his own created nature. Man is more than a physical being destined for annihilation. He is the object of divine interest, and his created nature is such that God's love abides with him. One can affirm that God will not at any time deal with man as an impersonal object. In saying that man should love himself, it is obvious that we are not approving selfishness or egocentricity. Inordinate self-love may be the root of all moral evil, as some writers have maintained. At any rate, inordinate self-love is contrary to genuine love for one's self.

Love of one's self is expressed in a variety of ways. I should like to suggest two apparent demonstrations. In the first place, the Christian should care for his body, since the body is the instrument through which one transfers his reverence for God to the manifold needs of men. For example, a Christian physician cannot allow his body to succumb to any form of dissipation. If he does so, his medical preparation, his deftness in performing his duties and his relations with his patients are impaired. As a Christian he should preserve his body to the best of his ability, for in doing so he preserves the instrument through which he mediates his interest in those whom he seeks to help. Likewise, a minister should exercise care in eating and drinking, and work and rest. Excessive concern for the integrity of the body, however, is uncalled for. A Christian must be prepared to sacrifice for the benefit of others. I mean by this that a disciplined routine must not be slavishly followed because the end sought is not the preservation of the body in the hope of a long life; the care of the body should be related to the office or the profession through which he ministers to the needs of man.

In the second place, the Christian should possess courage. One expresses his love for himself in his vigilant demonstration of courage. Courage is far more than sheer physical bravery. In fact, physical bravery may be nothing more than foolhardiness. Courage from a Christian point of view would signify a conquest over all impulses that would tend to belittle him. Moral cowardice is a constant threat that is conquered by strong convictions. The Christian, by his faith-commitment, sees moral cowardice as contrary to this commitment. Courage, by its very nature, involves risks that cannot be evaded in the social structure in which the Christian lives. Although it has just been observed that the Christian should care for his body, it does not follow that self-preservation should take precedence over courage.

It is impossible for one to love himself in the Christian sense and at the same time despise his neighbor or deal with him as less than God's person. As has been pointed out already, to love God is a sentiment of interest in the objects of God's love. It necessarily follows that the Christian should love his neighbor because his neighbor belongs to God.

How do we love our neighbors? First, love respects their individuality. Persons differ in physical appearance, mental ability, and in many other ways, but these differences are not the real constituents of persons. The distinguishing mark of a human being lies in the fact that he is the object of divine love and that he is created for fellowship. Inordinate self-love disregards and even despises this fact.

In the second place, love for our neighbors means an interest in all aspects of their well-being. The Christian certainly would seek to alleviate suffering, to eliminate injustices, to abolish discrimination, and to secure and guarantee to his neighbors the exercise of all their inalienable rights. Both individually and corporately, he would involve himself in these ends. It is for this reason that the individual Christian cooperates with the institutional church in its work through institutions of mercy and education for the benefit of man. These institutions have the right to be called Christian solely because the motivation for them is divine love, and because the end sought is the benefit of the objects of divine love. Without this motivation and without this interest in human benefit, there is nothing distinctive about these institutions. Love for God is always active in loving man.

In the third place, the Christian's love for his neighbors is a loving regard for their destiny. That is to say, his interest in them is not merely temporal. He is interested in their hearing the Word of God that redeems. Through his interest in their temporal welfare, he is expressing his gratitude for his own redemption and his confidence in the efficacy of the Word of God to deal adequately with all the menaces and perils of man. It is this confidence that gives impulse to his labors, for without this confidence temporal amelioration would be the only consequence of his interest. Thus, a loving regard for one's neighbors is ultimately a hope for Christian fellowship, a fellowship in the forgiveness of sin. The Christian's love for his neighbors transcends the visible and temporal works of his hands. These labors are token expressions of his interest in the communion of saints.

SUGGESTED READINGS

BEACH, WALDO. *The Christian Life*. Richmond: The Covenant Life Curriculum Press, 1966.

KNUDSON, ALBERT C. *Basic Issues in Christian Thought*. Nashville: Abingdon-Cokesbury Press, 1950. Chapter VI, 184-192.

MARSHALL, L. H. *The Challenge of New Testament Ethics*. New York: Macmillan and Company, Ltd., 1956. Chapter II, 32-62; Chapter IX, 278-316.

MATTSON, A. D. *Christian Ethics*. Rock Island: Augustana Book Concern, 1957. Chapter IX, 203-214.

NIEBUHR, REINHOLD. *An Interpretation of Christian Ethics*. New York: Harper and Brothers Publishers, 1935. Chapter VII, 199-220.

RAMSEY, PAUL. *Basic Christian Ethics*. New York: Charles Scribner's Sons, 1954. Chapters I, III; 1-46; 92-132.

DISCUSSION QUESTIONS

Chapter VI: THE CHRISTIAN'S LOVE

1. How does a Christian love God? Can a person love God only?

2. Does love for oneself involve him in egoism?

3. Can you love a person without liking him?

4. Can you love a person if you do not think he has personal value?

5. What are some manifestations of one's love for his neighbors?

GRATITUDE

GRATITUDE IS EVOKED. It can never be demanded, even by God. Genuine bestowal does not seek a recompense. If it be genuine bestowal, it is complete in itself and does not seek completeness in any demanded response.

If someone had told me on the day of my graduation from college that my parents were demanding my gratitude for financing my education, I would have known that I was being misinformed. Such a demand would have been contrary to their affection for their children as it had been expressed many times and in a variety of ways. Likewise, if someone should tell me that God demands my gratitude for his grace, I would know immediately that his conception of God did not stem from the revelation of God in Christ.

God's love for man is genuine love, without any alloy. This is the New Testament idea of *agape*. Love seeks the benefit of the beloved. It may well be that a grateful heart is pleasing to God. To urge that God demands gratitude would involve Him in egocentricity.

Gratitude for God's boundless love is evoked by the very nature of that love. Gratitude is not only an act of appreciation for the blessing received; it is also an evaluation of Him Who has given. Christian living is grateful living. It is a responsiveness that expresses itself in many ways.

In analyzing the Christian experience of gratitude, it is necessary to consider that for which the Christian is grateful. Man is a fragile creature continuously threatened by the world around him and poignantly aware of the inevitability of death. Existence is a frightening experience, for it is under the continuous threat of nonexistence. Man is a creature of suffering. In spite of his apparent health and in spite of the agility with which he moves, he is subject to pain and suffering. He may spend years attempting to master an instrument such as a violin, or he may spend many years attempting to develop adeptness in the use of a surgical instrument, or he may spend many years in studying the great literary classics, but all his skills and achievements are continuously imperiled by the possibility of injury to the body and by the certainty of death. These empirical facts cannot be evaded. They are both evident and insistent. Pessimism or a sense of futility has often resulted from an appraisal of man's frightful predicament.

Not only does threat arise from the physical world in which man lives, but also from the world of human relationships. It is not necessary to elaborate the point, for it is apparent that inordinate self-love has resulted in physical and emotional suffering. Social and economic injustices are rampant, and man's very existence on this planet is threatened by an immoral society.

The foregoing paragraphs have reference to man's physical and social involvements. Since man was created in the image of God, he is in a moral relationship with God. He is sinner. He is under judgment. This judgment speaks of death but

death here does not refer to annihilation; death here refers
to the separation from God that involves divine abhorrence
of sin and all that this abhorrence entails. Redemption signifies forgiveness of sin and, consequently, everlasting life
with God on the ground of His love.

It is bold to declare that Christ, the Word of God, has
related His redemptive activity to all aspects of evil that
threaten man. Commonly, Christ's redemptive activity has
been related to the salvation of the soul. If the soul should
be thought of as merely a part of a dual nature of man, then
Christ's redemptive work has reference only to a partial
salvation. It may well be, however, that when reference is
made to the salvation of the soul a complete redemption is
meant. This total adequacy of Christ's redemptive activity
must be made explicit, for Christ came to save man, the
whole man, from all evil regardless of its nature. It is important to juxtapose both the variety and the strength of
evil that threatens man and the inclusiveness of the redemptive activity of Christ. The real discernment and evaluation
of Christ's redemptive activity is a discernment and evaluation of the human plight from which He delivers man.

Thanks be to God! Gratitude is gratitude for something.
It is an evoked response. From all forms of evil in the world,
from breaches in human relationships and from moral guilt,
Christ has delivered us. Through His death and resurrection
every aspect of evil has been conquered, and wholeness of
life has been certified. This is the finality of revelation in
Him. The acts of dying and rising from the dead can be
located in history, but the redemptive purpose and significance transcend any moment of time. The work of redemption is finished, but some of the fruits and experiences of
that act lie in the future. The redemptive work of Christ is
the ground for hope. It is the impulse to activity by the
Christian in the world in which he lives for removing social

injustices, for caring for the sick and helpless, and for all forms of activity that are related to the Christian's love for his neighbors.

Gratitude is activity. It is an act in word and song, but it is more than these. It is a heart lifted to God in adoration; it is a hand extended in helpfulness. Here, as elsewhere, the inseparable relation between the vertical and the horizontal is apparent. It is here that faith and works are related. Lifted hearts of praise without extended hands of helpfulness are cold before God.

SUGGESTED READINGS

GARDNER, E. CLINTON. *Biblical Faith and Social Ethics.* New York: Harper and Brothers, 1960. Chapter VII, 161-166.

HARRINGTON, JOHN B. *Essentials in Christian Faith.* New York: Harper and Brothers, 1958. Chapter XIV, 195-208; Chapter XVIII, 258-272.

KAGAWA, TOYAHIKO. *Love, the Law of Life.* Philadelphia: The John C. Winston Company, 1929. Chapter VII, 125-136.

MATTSON, A. D. *Christian Ethics.* Rock Island: Augustana Book Concern, 1957. Chapter X, 224-246.

DISCUSSION QUESTIONS

Chapter VII: GRATITUDE

1. For what is the Christian grateful?

2. If gratitude is demanded from the recipient, what is the meaning of "gift?"

3. Why does Paul exhort Christians to give thanks? Are these exhortations to be understood as new demands?

4. Has a person accepted God's grace if he is not grateful for it?

5. Why would you say that gratitude for God's blessing is pleasing to him?

RESPONSIBILITY

IT HAS BEEN often said that responsibility is both the logical and moral deduction from privilege. This is not always the case, although in some instances, this relationship can be established. In considering the responsibility of the Christian, the relationship involves an important factor. It is the factor of voluntary acceptance of God's grace. Some examples may clarify the relation between acceptance and responsibility.

As a citizen of the United States, I have the privilege of moving from North Carolina to California. I could do so without asking permission from anyone. This privilege does not entail a responsibility. If I accept the privilege of establishing my residence in California, I accept all that residence there entails. Thus, it is in the acceptance of the privilege that responsibility arises. Or again, I have the privilege as an American citizen of securing a passport for sightseeing in Germany. The privilege, in and of itself, does not impose upon me any responsibility to go to Germany rather than to France or Spain. However, if I accept the privilege of visiting Germany, I come under the demands that the German government places upon its visitors. Or again, I have the privilege of owning and driving a car. The privilege itself does not impose upon me a responsibility for purchasing and driving a car; but if I do purchase and drive it, it is incumbent upon me that I obey the traffic laws.

And so it would seem that privilege and responsibility are related in some instances only when the privilege is exercised. Apart from the exercise of privilege, the demand of responsibility does not appear. Let me illustrate this further. In 1946, the President of Lenoir Rhyne College offered me a teaching position. I came to the college shortly thereafter for an interview. While I was on the campus, I heard bells ring in the corridors. These bells signified to me nothing more than that a class was over or a class was now to begin. I had the privilege of listening to these bells and of walking here and there without any sense of responsibility to the college. Later on, after I had accepted the offer to teach, these same bells signified something different. These bells told me that I must be in Room 1 to meet a class in Christian Ethics or in Room 2 to meet a class in Logic. It was in the acceptance of a teaching position that responsibility arose. Clearly, in this instance, the sense of responsibility inhered in the acceptance of the privilege.

The same relation exists between gratitude and responsibility for the Christian. Responsibility derives from gratitude and is inherent in it. Unless this relationship be clearly discerned, the sense of responsibility may be associated with demand, and, consequently, with law.

There is a sense in which gratitude is demanded. But the demand is not separable from the experience of gratitude itself. Reception of the gifts of God or response to the gifts of God are in themselves acts of gratitude. Response without gratitude is no response at all. Thus, it is in the inseparability of gratitude and response that it can be said that gratitude is demanded. When the Christian is reminded of his responsibility, he should not think that God is laying upon him some additional command that carries with it a threat for failure to meet the responsibility. When the Christian is reminded of his responsibility, he should reflect upon the inextricable relationship between gratitude and response and should search his heart to see what the natural expressions of gratitude are. If the Christian interprets responsibility as a form of moral coercion, he will still be under the demand of the law from which Christ has set him free. On the other hand, he will always be under the natural and glorious relationship between gratitude and responsibility, but he will not, thereby, experience legalistic demand.

The Christian is responsible for the proclamation of the gospel, but responsibility lies in the very acceptance of it. Responsibility is not additional to it; responsibility is not a legalistic adjunct. In the acceptance of the gospel, there is a stirring impulse to herald it. If this impulse to tell is absent, there has not been a genuine acceptance of the gospel. The commandment to preach the gospel to the world is not a legalistic demand laid upon the heart of the Christian; rather, it is the Lord's confirmation of the impulse to tell. The commandment is definitive of its scope and it authenticates the proclamation. The verbal command itself does not carry the impulse to tell. In this commandment our Lord validates the impulse to tell; *this impulse is already inherent in the Christian's acceptance of the gospel.* The Christian's proclamation of the gospel is an act of genuine fellowship with his Lord. Unless this inherent relationship is clearly understood, declarations of responsibility will be no more and no less than a new legalism.

It is important to distinguish between evangelical impulse and legalistic demand. The impulse to tell the gospel is

clearly an impelling response. Gratitude is more than an
emotion; it is an activity. Paul knew that his grateful response to Christ left him without any alternative than to
preach the gospel. There was an irresistible impulse within
him that made him say to himself, "Woe is unto me, if I
preach not the gospel!" (I Corinthians 9:16). He did not
know this as legalistic demand, but as impelling response.

The same experience came to early Christians who were
commanded to be silent regarding the gospel. They knew
that they could not be silent. "We cannot but speak of the
things we have heard and seen." Some of them said, "We
ought to obey God rather than men" (Acts 5:29). What
does *ought* mean here? Is it a legalistic demand? Not so!
It was a keen awareness of the impelling nature of response,
for without this inner impulse, they were poignantly aware
that they had not made a response to the gospel. Apart
from fellowship in Christ, "We ought to obey God rather
than men" is not an evangelical expression. In fellowship
with Him, "We ought to obey God rather than men" is insistent because it is inherent in response. Inherent response
effaces all elements of legalism.

The same is true with regard to Paul's use of the word
"slave." He referred to himself as the slave of Christ. The
analogy was taken from the then-current relation between
master and slave. "Slave" derived its meaning from the
manner in which the master beheld his slave. The master
possessed the slave who was subject to the will and whim
of his owner. The slave was in complete servitude to his
master. But Paul's use of the analogy must be seen from the
point of view of commitment. He interprets "slave" from
his awareness that he belongs to the Lord. The relationship
is that of a person committed to his Lord. His status is
that of willing devotion, a devotion that is known as impelling response. He knows that he belongs to Christ, and

Christ knows Paul as His forgiven friend and joint heir. Christ would not refer to Paul as His slave, but Paul would refer to himself as the slave of Christ. It is from this point of view that the analogy has meaning.

Responsibility from the evangelical point of view must always be seen as impelling response and never as legalistic demand. The nature of Christian fellowship necessitates this.

This inextricable relationship between gratitude and responsibility is illustrated in the concept of stewardship. This relationship is often overlooked, for the Christian is told that he must be a faithful steward. For example, he is told that everything belongs to the Lord and that he is entrusted with many and varied blessings, and consequently, must give an account of the manner in which he has used these gifts. He must give an account! Is this a new law, a legalistic demand? Not so! It is an explicit statement of a moral relationship. Let us pursue this a little further. Assuming that the Christian fulfills in every detail his responsibility as a steward, does he thereby merit a reward? Or does he become a better Christian? Obviously, a Christian is never a perfect steward. Does it follow that by the imperfect discharge of his stewardship he has failed as a steward and is thereby under the severity of condemnation? If the demand of stewardship is a legalistic demand, then his faithfulness in discharging it puts God under obligation to him, or failure puts him under condemnation before God. Thus, this interpretation of responsibility takes the Christian totally away from the gospel and places him anew under the demand of the law of sin and death.

Let us apply the evangelical principle to charity; in particular, let us apply it to tithing. It is the Christian's responsibility to give a tenth of his earnings, so we are told. If you do this, you are a Christian; consequently, God must reward you. If you do not do this, you are not Christian; conse-

quently, you are under condemnation, and this is highly
legalistic. But the evangelical approach to charity is one of
gratitude. It is an aspect of the impulse to tell the gospel,
for it is never unrelated to an interest in letting the world
know the Redeemer. And letting the world know that Christ
is the Redeemer manifests itself in a variety of ways, such
as the erection and maintenance of buildings of worship,
the support of educational institutions, provision for the
care of the sick and the aging, and in many other ways.
Christian giving of material substance is implicit in the
acceptance of the gospel. Christian giving is a responding
act that is inherent in being Christian. The evangelical approach to giving begins and ends in the giving of one's self
to the Lord. Thus the real response to the gospel is the
response of a person. Personal response to Christ seeks expression in giving, but no amount of giving by itself can
ever generate this personal response. Thus, the motive for
giving a tenth of one's income or any proportion of it does
not spring from a demand, but is inherent in this personal
relationship. Certainly, the Christian will desire to manifest
in monetary tokens and in other ways the actuality of the
giving of himself to his Lord.

Improper approaches to stewardship are both insipid and
misleading. It is utterly ridiculous to turn away from the
one and only motivation for stewardship to the banal and
trivial. This is too frequently done. For example, a man
attended a football game at which there were about 50,000
people. He estimated that each person had spent as much
as fifteen dollars for tickets and other expenses. He com-
pared the total amount with the frugality of gifts to the
church. Is this any more than an attempt to shame Christians
into giving to the Lord? Or, take this example that I recently
heard: so much is spent on cigarettes, snuff, cosmetics, soft
drinks, etc., and so little is given to the church. Shame on

you snuff-dippers! Shame on you rouge-wearers! Shame on you who try to slake your thirst with a cola. Insipid and misleading! Giving to the church that is prompted by such idiotic motivation is nothing short of a destruction of the gospel. The one and only genuine and approved Christian motivation for giving is the joyful self-giving of the redemptive Lord. Giving is a grateful response, and grateful response does not derive from any other source than the effectual hearing of the gospel. From a very practical point of view, insipid and misleading approaches to the stewardship of giving tend to empty the coffers of the church and, furthermore, tend to vitiate the gospel. It can be confidently affirmed that Christians, that is, those who have given themselves to the Lord and are grateful, will not allow the work of the church to go without adequate support. The only real interest of the church should be that of the proclamation of the gospel and the call to the world to hear it. Diligence here will never result in inadequate support, but the call to give that relates itself to any form of legalism becomes a hindrance to the work of the church and will ensnare the hearer through legalism. It must be strongly urged that responsibility in the area of stewardship is inseparably related to gratitude, and that Christ's redemptive work evokes that gratitude.

The preaching of responsibility does not stimulate a sense of responsibility. Such declarations are moralistic and devoid of the gospel. The Christian knows responsibility, but he knows this responsibility not as demand, but as impelling response. For example, John Doe is a Christian. In his pastor's sermon, the description is given of the direful plight of some 3,000,000 souls who are migratory laborers. Hearing this, as a Christian, he also hears the call to help. It is unnecessary for the minister to say, "This is your responsibility." Instead of saying, "This is your responsibility," it would be advisable for the minister to point out means by which the church can minister to these souls.

A personal experience may tend to clarify the misuse of responsibility within evangelical discourse. Some years ago I heard a Reformation sermon on "Justification by Faith." The minister affirmed that man is saved by (1) grace alone, (2) faith alone, (3) Christ alone and (4) the Scripture alone. The sermon up to this point was the *kerygma,* the proclamation of the gospel to me. I experienced then and there a deeper unworthiness; I knew then and there a heightened sense of the boundless and inscrutable love of God; I knew then and there an ecstasy of gratitude; I knew then and there an impulse to herald abroad by word and work this good news; I knew then and there that the Father had related Himself to me as His son. That was enough! Then the minister extinguished this divinely initiated response by deducing from God's gracious act a stern demand. He placed upon me a new demand that was more severe than the demand of the law from which Christ had set me free. I had already experienced what I have called elsewhere in this treatise an impelling response. His words were a legalistic demand which were totally alien to my response to the gospel and did violence to my relation to the Father as His son. When he added, "This is your responsibility," my heart was broken. For I found myself under a more severe inadequacy and condemnation. For I knew I was under a new legalism from which even Christ now could not set me free. If one really hears the gospel, this is response. To declare responsibility is external and additional to this response and is foreign to the reality of faith.

The point is clear. It may well be that responsibility is logically deduced from privilege. However, personal relationships do not fall within the scope of logical analysis. The proclamation of divine grace involves both God's judgment against the sinner and God's offer of unmerited favor for Christ's sake. The Christian's response of faith indicates both his concurrence in God's judgment and his apprehension of God's favor. This response is in itself an imperative, for responsive commitment involves both an abhorrence of sin and a dedication to the perfect imitation of Christ. If either element is eliminated from the foregoing description of grace, faith and responsive commitment, then a reinterpretation of these concepts would inevitably follow. To lay upon the Christian a legalistic demand that logically derives from divine favor severs the personal relationship that involves grace, faith, and responsive commitment. The demand of "responsibility" for benefit received can therefore be nothing short of a new legalism, a legalism that logically derives from grace. So grace that sets man free from the law of sin and death becomes the occasion for a more severe involvement in the very predicament from which he has been liberated. If responsibility is understood to be a logical deduction from grace, then the Christian is involved in the austerity of legalism. On the other hand, responsibility as impelling response indicates a moral relationship between the Christian and his Lord.

SUGGESTED READINGS

BONHOEFFER, DIETRICH. *Ethics.* Edited by Eberhard Bethge. New York: The Macmillan Company, 1955.

MARSHALL, L. H. *The Challenge of New Testament Ethics.* New York: The Macmillan and Company, Ltd., 1956. Chapter IV, 99-135.

MATTSON, A. D. *The Social Responsibility of Christians.* Philadelphia: Muhlenberg Press, 1960.

Note: See READING SUGGESTIONS for next chapter on "Duty."

DISCUSSION QUESTIONS

Chapter VIII: RESPONSIBILITY

1. How does response to the gospel relate to Christian responsibility?

2. Should Christian responsibility be looked upon as a logical deduction from grace?

3. What is the difference between accountability within fellowship with Christ and accountability outside of fellowship with Christ?

4. What is the distinction between impelling response and legalistic demand?

DUTY

PERSONAL PERFECTION THROUGH imitation of Christ has been made a moral ideal for the Christian. Is this a worthy goal? It is my opinion that this goal would tend toward spiritual pride. It would seem to me to be exceedingly difficult for this not to happen even when the perfection of Christ is made the norm. It would be better to say that the Christian strives for perfect imitation of Christ than to say that he strives for personal perfection through imitation of Him. The striving for perfect imitation would tend toward humility. Attention focused upon Christ would lead toward an ever increasing appraisal of His uniqueness as it was manifested in relation to His Father, to the historical situation in which He appeared, and to the persons with whom He lived. This uniqueness is His perfection.

Theologically, his moral perfection has been stated in the term sinlessness, for sinlessness expresses not only an absence of sin, but also an unswerving goodness or righteousness. Although the term itself be negative, the import of it is positive. The justification for the negative term lies in man's inability to define the nature of His perfection. Thus, a concentration of attention upon His personal perfection would result in deeper insight and appraisal. Christ grows! That is to say, His perfection continues to outrun the pace of human striving. Human insight grows, but it can never coincide with the perfection that Christ manifested.

This concentration upon Christ's personal perfection would make clear to the Christian the wide margin between his own imperfection and the perfection of Christ. And after all, why should the Christian seek personal perfection? Is he seeking a reward for meritorious living? He is already in fellowship with Christ and his foremost desire should not be that of personal perfection, for this would accent his own egocentricity. He is edified through Word and Sacrament. But this edification is within fellowship. The aim is not personal perfection as a meritorious achievement, although he does experience growth within this fellowship.

The knotty problem involved here lies in the Christian's attempt to relate the perfection which he finds in Christ to his own historical situation. Obviously, he cannot slavishly imitate Christ. The complex structure in which the Christian lives today is far removed from the simple structure of Christ's day. The wide divergence is too apparent to call for elaboration.

It is beyond the scope of this discourse to state the implications of the Christian's imitation of Christ. It is sufficient for our present purpose to say that the Christian who is in fellowship with Christ cannot be insensitive to the situation in which he lives. Callousness to his situation would indicate an insensitivity to Christ. And a precise delineation of the manner in which Christian sensitivity should express itself would deny the dynamic nature of personal fellowship.

It is at this very point that the nature of duty arises. Duty calls for interpretation from the point of view of fellowship in Christ. Duty is not an obligation laid upon the Christian for this would involve him again in legalism. Imposed duty disrespects relationship and is, therefore, a misinterpretation. Christian duty is inherent in Christian fellowship. Duty can never be effectually commanded. Awareness of duty as *ought* is nothing more than personal sensitivity within Christian fellowship. *Ought* does not signify external demand, but a sense of obligation generated by love itself. From this point of view, one could say that it was Christ's duty to love those who persecuted Him. Here it is apparent that duty for Him was not a foreign demand laid upon Him from without, but an obligation evoked by His fellowship with the Father. In like manner, Christian duty is an imperative within relationship and the imperative has no other origin than the fellowship itself.

From a practical point of view, duty can never be definitive. Duties vary from day to day for any individual, and duties are different for different individuals. In a broad sense, the only duty that every Christian has is that of being Christian and this duty, as has been pointed out, inheres in fellowship. In a strict sense, we cannot say that any one act is the duty of a particular Christian. He alone can say that. Discrete acts relate only to discrete persons. The individual's response within any given situation is primarily his response to God. It is his response in Christian fellowship to the external situation. And this response is the overt expression of fellowship in Christ.

Let us apply this evangelical principle to repentance and prayer. It has been said that repentance and faith are daily experiences of the Christian. These two words do not indicate two experiences. Repentance, if we can think of it apart from faith, plunges a person into the Slough of Despond. This sort of repentance, the Christian can never know. Repentance apart from faith is not repentance at all. And faith by its very nature involves repentance, for faith is a trustful uplift of the heart to the forgiving Lord. We cannot say to another Christian that it is his duty to repent; being Christian he knows this already. If he does not know it, telling him to do so will not cause him to repent.

Prayer is of the very essence of fellowship, for prayer is more than words addressed to God. It is communion of person with person. Thus, to say to a Christian that it is his duty to pray is to say to him that he is not a Christian. The Christian knows that he must pray because he is a Christian.

The application of this evangelical principle of duty thus becomes for the Christian his striving for perfect imitation of Christ. In no other way can the Christian know the real meaning of *ought* and in no other way can he effectually seek its application.

Two observations are pertinent at this point. In the first place, exhortation must not be misconstrued as imposed duty or legalistic demand. The Pauline Epistles are replete with exhortations to Christians to stand fast in their faith and to express their faith in godly living and charitable activity. Nowhere else in the New Testament does one find more vehement opposition to obedience to a demand as a means of meriting the favor of God than in the Pauline Epistles. Mutual exhortation among Christians is an expression of fellowship. It indicates both a reverence for God and an interest in the manifestations of Christian faith. Christian exhortation is an act that transcends selfish interest in personal salvation. Thus, exhortation is activated fellowship. Exhortations to prayer, repentance, serviceable activity, and faithfulness among Christians are a fervent desire that God's love be experienced and expressed in the fullest possible measure by all who are within the communion of saints. And this evangelical understanding removes exhortation from the realm of imposed duty.

In the second place, duty must not be construed as a logical deduction from grace. This is too frequently done. For example, this is done today by a misunderstanding of "cheap grace" and "cost of discipleship." Grace itself is cheap for it indicates a gift. It is costly to God if it be thought of in terms of the bitter suffering and death of Christ. It is not costly to God if it be thought of in terms of His nature as love. Love does not count the cost, but it rejoices in the blessing or benefit that it brings to the beloved. "Cheap grace," as the expression is commonly used, implies a demand that grace imposes upon the recipient. Thus, the acceptance of grace enforces upon the Christian the demand that he pay the cost of discipleship. The consequence is that artificial and self-imposed sacrifices are conjured up as means of repaying God for His grace. How erroneous! Whenever a Christian attempts to repay God by personal sacrifice, he is by this very act disavowing God's grace. On the other hand, by receiving God's grace as pure gift, the Christian is motivated and energized to strive for personal imitation of Christ. In doing so, it may be said that he pays the cost of discipleship. But one must exercise caution at this point. It is important to distinguish between the observer and the actor when making a judgment with regard to cost. As an observer, I could say that David Livingstone paid an exorbitant cost by going to Africa. As an actor, Livingstone adjudged the cost as negligible in comparison with the joy he experienced in serving his Lord. Whenever discipleship is a genuine response to grace, it is no longer measured in terms of personal cost. On the other hand, when there is a demand that the cost be paid, discipleship is no longer a response to grace, but it becomes a means for meriting grace. Duty is not a logical deduction from grace, but grace evokes gratitude and gratitude seeks expression. Thus, the Christian's awareness of duty is nothing more and nothing less than his impelling desire to glorify God by various manifestations of discipleship.

SUGGESTED READINGS

BARNETTE, HENLEE H. *Introducing Christian Ethics.* Nashville: Broadman Press, 1961. Chapter II, 19-25.

BONHOEFFER, DIETRICH. *The Cost of Discipleship.* New York: The Macmillan Company, 1958.

BRANSCOMB, HARVIE. *The Teachings of Jesus.* Nashville: Cokesbury Press, 1931. Chapter XIII, 195-211.

HARKNESS, GEORGIA. *Christian Ethics.* New York: Abingdon Press, 1957. Chapter VI, 104-121.

KNUDSON, ALBERT C. *Basic Issues in Christian Thought.* Nashville: Abingdon-Cokesbury Press, 1950. Chapter VI, 192-200.

MATTSON, A. D. *Christian Ethics.* Rock Island: Augustana Book Concern, 1957. Chapter IX, 215-223.

NIEBUHR, REINHOLD. *An Interpretation of Christian Ethics.* New York: Harper and Brothers Publishers, 1935. Chapter IV, 101-135.

SCOTT, ERNEST F. *The Ethical Teaching of Jesus.* New York: The Macmillan Company, 1949. Chapter XII, 83-88.

TITUS, HAROLD H. *Ethics for Today.* New York: American Book Company, 1947. Chapter IX, 137-152.

DISCUSSION QUESTIONS

Chapter IX: DUTY

1. Is the Christian ethic a perfectionistic ethic?

2. Why should the Christian strive for perfect imitation of Christ?

3. What difficulties are encountered in the attempt to imitate Christ?

4. Does failure to imitate Christ involve the Christian in guilt?

5. What is the source of the Christian's awareness of duty? In what sense is the awareness of duty an imperative?

6. Is duty for the Christian a logical deduction from grace?

7. How does Christian commitment relate to cost of discipleship?

8. Why is exhortation among Christians a vital aspect of their commitment to Christ? Are exhortations to be understood as demands?

Chapter X

JUSTICE

JUSTICE MUST BE properly interpreted. It has a distinctive meaning within the context of Christian fellowship. It is not analogous to civil justice, for civil justice has a different origin and intention. In courts of justice balance is sought between infraction of the law and penalty. The law whether it be Common Law or Statutory Law, is definitive both with respect to demand and sanction. Precedent in judgment also carries a sort of definitiveness. When any case is brought before a court of justice, the law is invoked as the standard by which the case in question is to be measured. And any judgment of infraction of the law carries with it the demand that the penalty be balanced with the degree and the seriousness of the guilt of the offender. That is to say, an attempt is made to balance penalty with infraction. For example, a person guilty of stealing a ham may be fined thirty dollars and the cost of the arraignment; for stealing a car, six months on the chain gang; for assault with a deadly weapon, three years in a penitentiary; and for income tax evasion, five years in a federal prison. This sort of retributive justice is arbitrary because penalties for similar offenses among the different nations of the world and even among the states that constitute the United States vary.

This sort of justice further signifies the punitive nature of law. The law is supported and ennobled through the infliction of some sort of punishment whether the punishment be a fine paid or an imprisonment endured. Payment of a fine or endurance of a punishment is looked upon as an eradication of guilt, for a person is no longer guilty before the law after payment has been made or after imprisonment has been endured. A stigma may attach itself to the reputation of the offender, but the law has no further grip on him; he has satisfied the sanction of the law.

The very fact that the Christian lives within such a legal arrangement gives rise to an uneasy conscience. He is subject to this law as a citizen, and by reason of this fact he participates in a corporate arrangement that offends his sensibility. Civil justice fails to recognize personal qualities that are paramount to the Christian, and it explicitly acknowledges punishment as an eradication of guilt. Punishment that is merely punitive, although it satisfies the demand of the law, may encourage further infractions by the very fact that punitiveness does not relate itself at all to the modification of the attitude of the offender. Law, although it may be necessary, cannot and does not heal. Retributive justice is an indictment of human nature. It stems from the empirical fact that man has not respected the inherent rights of his neighbor. Law may define the rights and privileges of persons. The empirical fact that every law carries with it the threat of punishment clearly indicates that the fear of punishment is the deterring motive. Law itself indicates the presence of evil and it seeks to overcome it by punitive measures. This fact is also demonstrated by the demand that a public example be made of the offender. The argument is that if any form of leniency be permitted, infractions

of the law will increase. Such an attitude does violence to
the nature of man. To make a public example of a person
does not express respect for him as a person.

Sanctions indicate retribution. It is "Eye for an eye and
tooth for a tooth." The sword of justice thus is retaliatory.
It cannot be otherwise since a definitive penalty indicates a
balance between the severity of the infraction and the
punishment for it. And since punishment is in itself punitive,
it is veritably *quid pro quo,* a quantum of punishment for
a degree of guilt.

Retaliation or retribution is alien to the Christian's understanding of love for his neighbor. Love cannot be vengeful.
Justice must be related to love. If justice be solidly fixed in
a forensic framework of retribution, it stands in stern opposition to love. Forensic exactness is by its very nature impersonal, whereas love, by its very nature, is personal. Forensic
exactness cannot issue in forgiveness, but love forgives. This
interpretation does not mean that offenders against law are
excused, nor does it mean that they are to be relieved of
punishment. It does mean that the punishment should be
removed from its mere punitivity.

Since the Christian is a historical person, he lives within
a legal structure. At the same time, however, he lives above
this structure by inveighing against mere punitiveness. He
has respect for the person who has offended and insists that
the offender be treated humanely. Thus, he would cry out
against cruel punishment. He would insist that any incarcer-
ated person be adequately clothed and fed, and he would
insist upon proper sanitation and medical care. Mere punishment violates the humanity of the offender.

In the second place, the Christian would urge that programs of rehabilitation be implemented. Not only would he
seek the rehabilitation of the offender with respect to citizen-
ship, but would provide for his spiritual needs. Such mea-

sures do not derive from law and its threatened penalty. Where programs of rehabilitation and spiritual concern are evident, the motivation has not derived from jurisprudence. It has its origin elsewhere. Love abides, and one meaning of this is that love never exhausts itself. Love must accompany the guilty and seek their recovery.

The upsurge of interest in social justice is apparent. This striving for social justice has expressed itself in a variety of ways. Organizations seeking justice for deprived persons are numerous. Vociferous demands for laws to protect ethnic groups have had telling effect. Civil rights are being urged on the ground that justice must respect inalienable rights. The Christian must be cognizant of this demand and he can do no less than insist that the inalienable rights of all persons regardless of their race, color, economic status, and social attitude be respected. His interpretation of inalienable, however, is crucial. Social justice urges the abolition of privation and pain, of discrimination in job opportunities, and an end to racial oppression. These evils, it is maintained, are unjust and must be eradicated. Justice is here related to balance. The dispossessed do not deserve the punishment that is inflicted upon them by discriminatory actions and privations nor do the perpetrators of injustice deserve the rewards of their iniquity.

Sympathy for the dispossessed seems to be the motive for rectifying the situation. This form of humaneness is not to be despised, but it is highly inadequate. The motive for rectification should not derive from pity; genuine rectification does not express itself solely in the right to vote, the right to a job, the right to associate freely, and the right to open housing. These rights are not unworthy ends, but they should be related to a higher end. The Christian motivation does not spring from sympathy or empathy, nor does it seek the mere rectification of these social and economic injustices.

The Christian's motivation is divine love that recognizes every person as God's person. The Christian's love extends to all persons, and he is hurt by the fact that others suffer. He seeks their complete wholeness in the love of God. His efforts, although they may be expressed in demands for civil rights, spring from his awareness of God's love for all mankind and his appraisal of all persons as belonging to God. His efforts are expressions of his fellowship with God through the redemptive activity of Christ, and are no less than a glorification of God through imitation of His redemptive activity. His efforts are an attempt to apply the gospel to the varying needs of man. Regardless of the form that they may take, they are an expression of his confidence in redemptive love. Inalienable rights inhere in the created nature of man as image of God and in the right that every man has to hear the gospel.

When the Christian struggles for civil rights, he acts from the only complete motivation. That motivation is divine love. Mere rectification of social injustice is not a worthy end. The only worthy end is the enrichment of life both horizontally and vertically.

In person-to-person relationships, love must rise above retaliation and vengefulness. It does not minimize the seriousness of any form of sin, and it does not pass final judgment. Love is communicative, and the end it seeks is fellowship. Forgiveness does not signify forgetfulness; it signifies a desire for the removal of the breach that separates the offended from the offender. The Christian forgives his enemy because he desires him as his friend. If the enemy hungers, let him starve if you want him to remain your enemy. If he hungers, feed him if you want him as your friend. The Christian does not forgive because he underestimates the seriousness of that which is done against him. He forgives because he is forgiven. He seeks the enrichment

of the fellowship of Christ by extending this fellowship even
to his enemy. Justice for him can never mean a balancing
of the severity of an offense with retaliation. Love rises
above vengefulness and thereby heals.

Self-preservation has been urged by some as the first
law of nature. This may or may not be true if it is related
only to physical preservation. It is true as a Christian relates
it to himself. In the very act of love for his neighbors he
knows a kind of self-preservation; he knows that his relation
to Christ cannot be preserved through vengefulness. But
this is not selfishness; it only affirms that love is lost if and
when it ceases to love. Self-preservation was vital to the
suffering Christ in Gethsemane. It was not fear of suffering
and dying that produced the bloody sweat. He knew that
He must die; either one death or another stood before Him.
He could have returned from Gethsemane to Nazareth and
lived out a normal life; in so doing love would have died.
In standing His ground, He was reaffirming the love that
spoke and worked. And thus He died on a cross. Death
preserved! In like manner there is self-preservation in self-
effacement. And it is in this very self-effacement that love
finds its strongest arm of fellowship.

Since love is communicative, it cannot be retained by the
lover. It has meaning only when it is expressed. Love unites
the recipient with the lover. Love becomes a kind of dis-
tributed justice that recognizes every person as belonging to
God. Thus, when justice is detached from love, it is fixed
within the inexorable bond of demand and punishment.
Love relates justice to persons.

SUGGESTED READINGS

AULEN, GUSTAF. *Church, Law and Society.* New York: Charles Scribner's Sons, 1948. Chapter IV, 75-92.

FLETCHER, JOSEPH. *Situation Ethics.* Philadelphia: The Westminster Press, 1966. Chapters V, VI, 87-119.

NIEBUHR, REINHOLD. *An Interpretation of Christian Ethics.* New York: Harper and Brothers Publishers, 1935. Chapter VIII, 221-237.

RAMSEY, PAUL. *Basic Christian Ethics.* New York: Charles Scribner's Sons, 1954. Chapter VII, 234-248.

TITUS, HAROLD H. *Ethics for Today.* New York: American Book Company, 1947. Chapter XV, 225-238.

DISCUSSION QUESTIONS

Chapter X: JUSTICE

1. Do you accept the idea that justice is love distributive?

2. Is there a parallel between civil justice and the justice of God?

3. Is the petition, "Forgive us our debts as we forgive our debtors" related to distributive justice?

4. Should confrontation or gradualism be the policy of the Christian with respect to civil injustice?

5. Can a person be both just and forgiving?

Chapter XI

FREEDOM

IN ORDER TO demonstrate the nature of Christian freedom, it would be profitable to examine some deterministic points of view.

In the first place, there is theological determinism. This form of determinism posits certain attributes of God such as omnipotence, omniscience, and goodness. Since He is omniscient, He knows all there is to be known; since He is omnipotent, there is no other power than His own. Omniscience and omnipotence combine to fix all events; consequently, there is an absolute determinism. If He is good, it follows that any form of evil regardless of its nature cannot have had its origin in Him. And since He is omniscient and omnipotent, evil does not have an origin apart from Him. But He is good. Since He is good, it follows that every act of omnipotence and omniscience is good and God is the efficient cause of sin. Since the attributes of omnipotence, omniscience, and goodness are unvarying an absolute determinism ineluctibly follows. Both a pre-determinism with respect to all cosmic and personal events and a pre-destina-

100

tion with respect to every person cannot be logically evaded.

Moreover, fixing upon such attributes as omnipotence, omniscience, and goodness eliminates freedom and reinterprets evil, as it is viewed by man, as an indispensable element of divine goodness. Thus evil is not in reality evil; it is only so through man's misinterpretation of it. It is good that evil exists because God has ordained it.

Attempts have been made to resolve the problem of freedom that is inherent in this approach by distinguishing between God's fore-knowledge and His fore-ordination. But it has been maintained that such a distinction limits God. To fore-know, if He be omniscient, and to fore-ordain, if He be omnipotent, would clearly indicate an absolute actuality in every detail. For if He knows all things and does not fore-ordain them, there is a form of inactuality in His nature. Fore-knowledge and fore-ordination express a distinction in words, but lack any real distinction as they relate to the nature of God. Furthermore, it has been maintained that this distinction is a heuristic device to afford a person some ground for saying that he is free to make choices.

Fixing upon abstract attributes is the approach of definition to actuality. But this is not the proper approach. This approach is abstract and the logical consequences of these abstractions cannot result in anything else than an abstract conception of deity. From the evangelical point of view, we do not understand God in terms of abstract attributes, but by means of God's revelation of Himself in Christ. If we begin by fixing upon certain abstract attributes and reify them as unvarying and indispensable, an absolute predetermination and predestination must be affirmed. But we must interpret these attributes in the light of revelation in Christ as activities belonging to God. To detach these attributes and to define them as mere attributes is one thing, but to interpret these attributes as qualities of activity in the revealed God is another.

Who is God? The Christian knows God through His redemptive activity in Christ. He does not come to a knowledge of Him through ratiocination. The Christian trusts God because God has redeemed him. He does not trust God because he conceives of God as having fixed attributes. The Christian lives in the assurance of hope, for the integrity of God finds its only certification in God's redemptive activity. He does not rest his hope upon some abstract conception of divine attributes. The Christian lives in this redemptive relationship and, consequently, knows God within the relationship that God by His own will and activity has established. If one knows God within this personal relationship, it would follow that the attributes of God are not abstractions; they are a delineation of personal activity. This is quite different from a delineation of abstract attributes that combine to form an abstract conception of deity.

Christian freedom is freedom within fellowship. Here again we do not begin with a conception but with a relationship. An abstract concept of freedom would involve all sorts of rational difficulties. It is the freedom that is generated by fellowship through the forgiveness of sin that is pivotal here. The accent is this: The Christian is free to live as a Christian. It is this personal relationship that establishes him in freedom.

Sin enslaves. Sin is estrangement from God. God's gracious Act in Christ destroys this alienation and brings freedom. Grace through the activity of the Holy Spirit evokes faith. Now through faith one is free to love God, free to love himself, and free to love his fellow man. This freedom is the only real freedom that has ultimate meaning. In this freedom the Christian lives and moves. It is freedom within commitment. On the one hand, God has committed Himself in the abundance of His love even unto death upon a cross.

On the other hand, the Christian has committed himself to this gracious work of redemption by apprehending through faith as the Holy Spirit has effectually worked in him. It is within this commitment that the Christian, as a historical person, makes his particular decisions and choices. It is not particular decisions and choices that are of primary importance in the consideration of freedom. Of primary importance is the relationship with God in which the particular decisions and choices are made. Apart from the forgiveness of sin, moral choices and decisions cannot liberate man from his alienation nor do they express genuine freedom. Paradoxically, the Christian is free as he is captive to the love of God in Christ. His highest freedom is in his complete yielding to that love. And it is in this acknowledgment of sovereign lordship that he is free, free as a Christian and free to live as a Christian.

Mechanistic determinism may be cited as a second form. The world is like a machine. Cause and effect are unbroken. Every effect has its antecedent cause, and every cause produces an inevitable effect. Every cosmic event is determined by its cause; every cosmic event is a prediction of its consequence. Indeterminism is absolutely disallowed. For example, if one had full knowledge of the weather today, of the temperature, barometric pressure, force and direction of wind, and all other elements which constitute the weather, he could foretell with accuracy the weather for any future date. Future cosmic events are in actuality past events finding expression in future events. Future events are hermetically sealed in their antecedents.

From the point of view of the evangelical conception of life, several comments are pertinent. This inextricable relationship between cause and effect signifies for the Christian the orderly manner with which God governs His cosmos. This principle of causation indicates His unswerving control of all that He has created. Causation is not an efficient principle, but it is an ordered activity, and this ordered activity is an evidence of God's dependability. Events do not produce events, but God rules the world. He watches over His creation, and He is its source and energy.

Confidence in the dependability of God is the ground for any inquiry by the Christian into the nature of the created order. On the basis of observation and experimentation, laws of nature can be formulated. The formulations of these laws of nature express confidence in this dependability. An inquiry into the nature of the world in which the Christian lives is an act of faith in God, the Father, Creator of Heaven and earth. This interpretation of natural law is not objectionable to the Christian. The principle of causation is understood as an expression of the manner in which God ceaselessly engages Himself in His rulership of His created order. Obviously, this is not materialistic mechanism, for matter is not the primary or primordial substance; God is the Creator and ruler of the universe. This is one way of affirming both the transcendence and the immanence of God.

On this ground, inquiry into the nature of things is not only an act of faith that indicates a confidence in God's dependability; it is also an act of worship. Respect for God's created order derives from this understanding. The Christian is free to inquire into the nature of the constituents of the world and into the interrelatedness of discrete elements in it, and he is free to use them with trustful and worshipful discretion. In so doing, he glorifies God.

In the third place, there is psychological determinism. The argument can be expressed in the following manner. An individual did not choose his parents; consequently, there is a fixed heredity. He did not choose the location of his birth nor the domestic, economic, social, and cultural milieu; consequently, there is a fixed environment. The experiences that came to him through the impact of physical events and from contact with other persons were beyond his control. At no point in his life did he select the events and human influences that touched him. The totality of influences imperceptibly molded him and thereby determined his personality. Declaration that he is free is a mere declaration; it indicates nothing more or less than that he is conscious of his actions. But every seeming choice is predetermined by the seeming choices in a series of determined actions.

The Christian is a historical person. He lives in a world of things, events, and persons. He is sensitive to his environment. He does respond and react. If this is denied, a reinterpretation of the nature of man would be required. It is true that he does not create his environment, and it is true that he does not order the words and actions of others. There is no way by which he can predict with any degree of accuracy the events that will unfold before him in his future nor can he predict what he will say or do at any moment in his own future. He lives in this world as a person.

The crucial point is clear. Does the external world of objects, events, and persons totally determine his personality and, thereby, obviate his freedom?

The evangelical conception of life affirms that God has revealed Himself to sinful man and that the final revelation of Him is His redemptive activity in Christ. This revelation is to sinful man. Sin, whether it be spoken of as act or state, signifies some form of estrangement from God. It is absurd to urge that an estranged person would initiate the elimination of his own estrangement. To urge that an estranged person would love God or even seek to love Him is equally absurd.

The environment of the Christian involves more than the horizontal relations of his life. He does live on the horizontal plane of physical objects, events, and personal relationships.

He lives also in the personal relationship of Father to son, the relationship of fellowship in the forgiveness of sin. His environment at any point in his life involves both his relationship to God and the totality of his horizontal relations. If only the horizontal influences are considered, then the most vital element in his relationship is disregarded. He does not merely react to horizontal impact. Such limited analysis of his response is a denial of his created nature. It may well be that a person is totally determined if he is merely a creature responding to his horizontal environment. But the evangelical understanding of man disallows this. In fellowship with God, a fellowship in the forgiveness of sin, the Christian makes his response to the horizontal environment. It is at this point that he is aware of his freedom. To put it sharply, he expresses his fellowship with God through the choices he makes in the world of persons and events. He is free to be a Christian. It does not profit a great deal to analyze the abstract concept of the freedom of the will, for such an analysis so often leaves the mind of man tied in a rational knot. In Christ, man knows that he is free.

In speaking of the freedom of the Christian, I am not attempting to deal with the philosophical problem of the freedom of the will. The scope of this discourse is limited to the freedom of the Christian who is in fellowship with Christ.

It is highly important at this point to make two distinctions. In the first place, the Christian knows that God has elected him. That is to say, God has chosen him through the call of the gospel. I must be careful to say that I am not discussing here the doctrine of election, for this treatise deals only with the life of the Christian. Although he may be aware that the good news has effectually come to him, he does not conclude from this experience any limitation upon the activity of God on other lives in the past or in the present.

Election as I have used it here is restricted to the life of him who is in fellowship with Christ. He affirms by his act of faith that he is a forgiven sinner and, consequently, that God has chosen him in Christ. Thus, the primary decision, if we can speak of God as making a decision, is God's decision in favor of him. To reiterate, this does not mean that God has failed to choose others. It means simply and nothing more than the Christian knows through the forgiveness of sin God's favor upon him.

The other part of the primary decision is the commitment of faith. The Christian responds to God's election. The Christian knows that he did not choose God, but that God chose him in Christ. His choice of God was an awakened response, a response that he did not initiate, and a response that he did not by his own volition create. His response was his own. It was his own because it was not coerced, although it was provoked by divine love.

The call of the gospel was a call to liberation, for the call of the gospel was an invitation to the destruction of estrangement. Why the Christian responded to this call while other persons rejected it is beyond the scope of this analysis. A troublesome problem is not being dismissed, but merely recognized as one of many inexplicable reactions to the call of the gospel.

The particular decisions of a Christian, hence, are secondary. He continues to make decisions throughout his life. But these decisions are made within the primary decision, the primary decision being God's election of him in Christ and his own commitment of faith.

In the second place, it is important to distinguish between freedom in fellowship and freedom outside of fellowship. Freedom within fellowship is restricted by reason of the commitment of faith. Thus, the question of whether a person is free to become a Christian is not being dealt with, but the freedom of him who has responded to God's election is under consideration. The debilitating consequences of original sin or the intransigency of the will because of total depravity, if such opinions are upheld by the reader, are not points for discussion. The point is that the Christian is in fellowship and that he is free as a Christian.

This freedom is quite frequently overlooked. When freedom is discussed, accountability is frequently stressed. Accountability outside of fellowship is not the same as accountability within fellowship. Accountability outside of fellowship involves a judgment of God that does not relate to grace. God's judgment of the Christian is a judgment within grace, and any error that the Christian makes in discrete decisions is a judgment within grace and, consequently, is not a judgment of condemnation. The frightfulness of error is not minimized, for a Christian lives in the mood of repentance and faith constantly. Thus, accountability must not be associated with condemnation; it must always be associated with forgiveness.

Erroneous decisions do not mark a flouting of the divine will; they indicate an imperfection in choice. The Christian strives for a perfect imitation of Christ. Decisions that mark a failure to imitate Him are not decisions against Christ, but they are indications of human fraility. Outside of Christ, errors do not signify this. Outside of Christ, errors signify unbelief or antagonism.

Christ has set the Christian free. He is free from the law of sin and death. Now he is free in the law of nature and necessity. The only genuine freedom is freedom within the law of love. It is within this law of love that he moves freely in the decisions of life.

SUGGESTED READINGS

DEWEY, ROBERT E. AND GOULD, JAMES A. *Freedom: Its History, Nature and Varieties.* London: The Macmillan Company, 1970. Part 3, "Freedom of the Will," 103-162.

GARDNER, E. CLINTON. *Biblical Faith and Social Ethics.* New York: Harper and Brothers, 1960. Chapter VII, 170-174.

KNUDSON, ALBERT C. *Basic Issues in Christian Thought.* Nashville: Abingdon-Cokesbury Press, 1950. Chapter II, 51-86.

LUTHER, MARTIN. *Works of Martin Luther.* Translated by W. A. Lambert. Philadelphia: A. J. Holman Company, 1916. "A Treatise on Christian Liberty," 312-348.

NIEBUHR, H. RICHARD. *Christ and Culture.* New York: Harper and Brothers, 1951. Part VII, Chapter IV, 249-256.

RAMSEY, PAUL. *Basic Christian Ethics.* New York: Charles Scribner's Sons, 1950. Chapter II, 46-91.

SCOTT, ERNEST F. *Man and Society in the New Testament.* New York: Charles Scribner's Sons, 1947. Chapter IX, 226-254.

TITUS, HAROLD H. *Ethics for Today.* New York: American Book Company, 1947. Chapter VII, 104-114.

TITUS, HAROLD H. *Living Issues in Philosophy.* New York: American Book Company, 1964. Chapter XI, 183-201.

DISCUSSION QUESTIONS

Chapter XI: FREEDOM

1. What objections do you offer to theological determinism?

2. What objections do you offer to psychological determinism?

3. What objections do you offer to mechanistic determinism?

4. What do you understand by freedom of the will?

5. How does the question of freedom relate to the nature of sin?

6. Apart from forgiveness of sin, is a person free to love God and his neighbor?

7. Can a person ever become free by obedience to law? Is freedom prior to obedience?

Chapter XII

OBEDIENCE

AN ANALYSIS OF *Love Activates and Acts* would be incomplete without a discussion of obedience, for obedience is the hallmark of Christian living. I have reserved the analysis of obedience for this final chapter because it signifies moral activity that relates to each of the preceding discussions. A treatment of obedience, therefore, properly concludes this book.

Obedience exists within relationship and it is activity within relationship. The Christian is related to God as son to Father. And his obedience is a recognition of this relationship in his decisions and actions. Obedience is a filial response to God through the manner of life that is pleasing to Him.

"God was in Christ, reconciling the world unto himself" (II Corinthians 5:19). This passage is profoundly simple. Here is a message that the least literate can understand and that the most scholarly theologian cannot comprehend. It contains the essentials that relate to salvation and to the final revelation of God in Christ. Every aspect of evangelical theology and ethics rests upon this work of Christ.

> For by grace are ye saved through faith; and that not
> of yourselves; it is the gift of God; Not of works, lest
> any man should boast. For we are his workmanship,
> created in Christ Jesus unto good works, which God
> hath before ordained that we should walk in them
> (Ephesians 2:8-10).

Herein is the basis for the evangelical doctrine of justification
by faith. It can be affirmed that obedience has nothing to
do with salvation. A person is not saved because he obeys;
obedience is not the cause of salvation. The Christian obeys
because he is saved.

"For it is God which worketh in you both to will and to
do of his good pleasure" (Philippians 2:13). Obedience is
expressive of relationship. God reconciles through the death
of His Son. It is God who "Called me through the Gospel,
enlightened me by His gifts, and sanctified and preserved
me in the true faith" (Luther's explanation, third article of
the Creed). God incites and energizes Christian obedience.

Obedience is an act of reverence. It has respect for the
majesty of God's love. It is a reverential regard for Him Who
is holy.

Obedience is an act of worship. It is by its very nature an
act of communion with God. Obedience that does not adore
is foreign to impelling response.

Obedience is natural. The law of sin and death was abrogated by Christ and the law of nature and necessity was
fulfilled by Him. Christ has not delivered man from the
law of nature and necessity, the law of love; man has been
re-established within this law of his being. Obedience to
God, hence, is not contrary to man's created nature because
it is the true expression of his authentic self. This point cannot be too strongly urged. If obedience is unnatural, it is
not expressive of fellowship. Obedience, then, would be

derived from a demand that is foreign to fellowship.

Although obedience is natural, the Christian does not obey perfectly. He is fallible and herein lies the cause for continuous repentance. Repentance itself indicates the unnaturalness of sin. If sin be natural, Christ's victory over sin would have been the conquering of that which is according to nature. But Christ has conquered sin, and the Christian is a Christian through grace. He is not a Christian because of perfect obedience, but he strives through the Holy Spirit to obey.

Obedience is an act of gratitude. "We love Him, because He first loved us" (I John 4:19). We obey Him because He first loved us. The Christian obeys because he is grateful for God's love, and this gratitude is a genuine motive for obedience.

Obedience is a good disposition toward God. It is opposite to antagonism, rejection, or defiance. It signifies acceptance of and concurrence in God's will, and it signifies a delight to do His will. Christian obedience is not conformity to a legalistic demand, but is expressive of fellowship.

The Christian is inquisitive. He seeks to know the will of God. He desires to be spiritually informed. The Christian studies the Bible, listens to the preaching of the gospel and worships God. The Christian desires to know more about human relationships in order to relate the will of God to the needs of man. Inquisitiveness is an act of obedience.

Only in freedom can obedience be dynamic. When obedience is disconnected from freedom, both obedience and freedom are misunderstood. From the evangelical point of view, freedom constitutes the moral realm in which obedience can be expressed.

Only love can obey. Obedience is devoid of motivation apart from evoked love. This is what Paul means when he says:

> Owe no man any thing, but to love one another; for
> he that loveth another hath fulfilled the law. For this,
> Thou shalt not commit adultery. Thou shalt not kill,
> Thou shalt not steal, Thou shalt not bear false witness,
> Thou shalt not covet; and if there be any other com-
> mandment, it is briefly comprehended in this saying,
> namely, Thou shalt love thy neighbour as thyself.
> Love worketh no ill to his neighbour; therefore love is
> the fulfilling of the law (Romans 13:8-10).

The only law that love can fulfill is the law of love, the
law that is inherent in the nature of God and in the created
nature of man. This is true because God is love. Both the
motive and the dynamic for loving Him spring from His
nature. This is also true because man who is created in the
image of God is created in love, to love, and for love. It is
from this evangelical truth that responsibility, duty, and
obedience must be understood.

The frightful nature of sin lies in the fact that it is a
denial of the nature of God and a rejection of the nature of
man. Sin indicates a rupture in the relation between man
and God. Forgiveness of sin overcomes this rupture and
signifies a revitalization of man. In this revitalization the
Christian is free to love God, to love himself, and to love
his fellow man. As a forgiven sinner, he lives and moves
within the law of love. Only within this law of love is obedience possible. Obedience has reverential regard for God who
is love. It is both an attitude and an activity expressing one's
authentic self.

SUGGESTED READINGS

ELERT, WERNER. *The Christian Ethos.* Translated by Carl
J. Schindler. Philadelphia: The Muhlenberg Press, 1957.
Chapter VII, 240-282.

ENSLIN, MORTON SCOTT. *The Ethics of Paul.* New York:
Harper and Brothers Publishers, 1930. Chapter X, 231-294.

KIERKEGAARD, SOREN. *Works of Love.* Translated by David
and Lillian Swenson. Princeton: Princeton University
Press, 1946. Volume I, Chapter III, 75-124.

RAMSEY, PAUL. *Basic Christian Ethics.* New York: Charles
Scribner's Sons, 1950. Chapter IX, 337-342.

STRUMP, JOSEPH. *An Explanation of Luther's Small Cate-
chism.* Philadelphia: The United Lutheran Publication
House, 1907. Part I, "The Ten Commandments," 39-77.

DISCUSSION QUESTIONS

Chapter XII: OBEDIENCE

1. Is obedience a means to salvation?

2. Why must the Christian be obedient to his Lord?

3. Is obedience to God's will possible apart from love of God?

4. Is obedience primarily an act or an attitude?

5. Why can it be said that love is the fulfillment of the law?

TE DEUM GLORIA

IN THE INTRODUCTION I stated the situations in which the Christian lives. Now I wish to conclude this brief treatise by summarizing the evangelical view of life. I shall do so by appropriate quotations.

I. THE EVANGELICAL COMMENDATION

"God is love" (I John 4:16).

"For God so loved the world, that he gave his only begotten Son, that whosoever believeth in him should not perish, but have everlasting life"
(John 3:16).

"God was in Christ, reconciling the world unto himself" (II Corinthians 5:19).

"But God commendeth his love toward us, in that, while we were yet sinners, Christ died for us"
(Romans 5:8).

II. THE EVANGELICAL CONFIDENCE

"For by grace are ye saved through faith; and that not of yourselves: it is the gift of God"
(Ephesians 2:8).

"For I am persuaded, that neither death, nor life, nor
angels, nor principalities, nor powers, nor things
present, nor things to come, nor height, nor depth,
nor any other creature, shall be able to separate us
from the love of God, which is in Christ Jesus our
Lord" (Romans 8:38-39).

III. The Evangelical Commission

"But ye shall receive power, after that the Holy Ghost
is come upon you: and ye shall be witnesses unto
me both in Jerusalem, and in all Judea, and in Sama-
ria, and unto the uttermost part of the earth"
(Acts 1:8).

"Go ye into all the world, and preach the gospel to
every creature" (Mark 16:15).

IV. The Evangelical Exhortation

"Whether therefore ye eat, or drink, or whatsoever ye
do, do all to the glory of God" (I Corinthians 10:31).

"I beseech you therefore, brethren, by the mercies of
God, that ye present your bodies a living sacrifice,
holy, acceptable unto God, which is your reasonable
service. And be not conformed to this world: but
be ye transformed by the renewing of your mind,
that ye may prove what is that good, and acceptable,
and perfect, will of God" (Romans 12:1-2).

"Therefore, my beloved brethren, be ye stedfast, un-
moveable, always abounding in the work of the
Lord, forasmuch as ye know that your labour is
not in vain in the Lord" (I Corinthians 15:58).

V.   THE EVANGELICAL TRIUMPH

"Rejoice in the Lord alway: and again I say, Rejoice.
Let your moderation be known unto all men. The
Lord is at hand. Be careful for nothing; but in every
thing by prayer and supplication with thanksgiving
let your requests be made known unto God. And
the peace of God, which passeth all understanding,
shall keep your hearts and minds through Christ
Jesus" (Philippians 4:4-7).

"Peace I leave with you, my peace I give unto you:
not as the world giveth, give I unto you. Let not
your heart be troubled, neither let it be afraid"
                                    (John 14:27).

"But now is Christ risen from the dead, and become
the firstfruits of them that slept. For since by man
came death, by man came also the resurrection of
the dead. For as in Adam all die, even so in Christ
shall all be made alive. But every man in his own
order: Christ the firstfruits; afterward they that
are Christ's at his coming" (I Corinthians 15:20-23).

VI.   THE EVANGELICAL SONG

Jesus, Master, Whose I am,
    Purchased, Thine alone to be,
By Thy Blood, O spotless Lamb,
    Shed so willingly for me,
Let my heart be all Thine own,
Let me live for Thee alone.

Other lords have long held sway:
    Now, Thy Name alone to bear,

Thy dear voice alone obey,
   Is my daily, hourly prayer:
Whom have I in heaven but Thee?
Nothing else my joy can be.

Jesus, Master, I am Thine:
   Keep me faithful, keep me near;
Let Thy presence in me shine,
   All my homeward way to cheer.
Jesus, at Thy feet I fall,
O be Thou my all in all.

Jesus, Master, Whom I serve,
   Though so feebly and so ill,
Strengthen hand and heart and nerve
   All Thy bidding to fulfill;
Open Thou mine eyes to see
All the work Thou hast for me.

Lord, Thou needest not, I know
   Service such as I can bring;
Yet I long to prove and show
   Full allegience to my King.
Thou an honor art to me;
Let me be a praise to Thee.

Jesus, Master, wilt Thou use
   One who owes Thee more than all?
As Thou wilt! I would not choose;
   Only let me hear Thy call.
Jesus, let me always be
In Thy service glad and free.

(Frances Ridley Havergal, 1865)

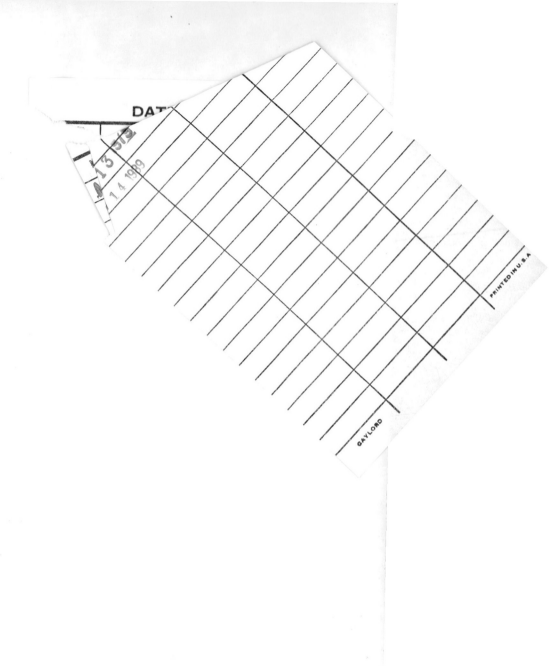